Yes, You Can Write

and here's how...

A Red Stag guide to everyday writing

David Rice

Published in 2018 by:
RED STAG
(a Mentor Books imprint)
Mentor Books Ltd
43 Furze Road
Sandyford Industrial Estate
Dublin 18
Republic of Ireland

Tel: +353 1 295 2112 / 3
Fax: +353 1 295 2114
Email: admin@mentorbooks.ie
Website: www.mentorbooks.ie

A CIP catalogue record for this title is available from the British Library.

ISBN 978-1-912514-29-8

Cover Design: Anú Design
Visit our websites: www.mentorbooks.ie
                     www.redstag.ie

Based on the notes from the Killaloe Hedge-School of Writing

FOR almost 20 years people have come from a total of 19 countries worldwide to the weekend and one-day workshops of the Killaloe Hedge-School of Writing (KHS). It has resulted in many hundreds of newspaper and magazine articles, more than 100 published books (both fiction and non-fiction, including best-sellers) and even international fame for some of the 'alumni'. There has been such a demand for the summary notes from the workshops (even to the point that certain lecturers elsewhere have photocopied these notes and issued them as their own, deleting the logo and the copyright notice), that we have decided to develop them into a series of small writing guides, courtesy of Red Stag publishers—

Yes, You Can Write

Start that Novel

Write a Memoir

The Non-Fiction Book

The Rathmines Stylebook (updated)

This is the first of them. It is our hope that these little books will be as helpful to the thousands of folks who would love to write, as the Killaloe Hedge-School of Writing workshops have been. *(www.Killaloe.ie/khs)*

~ David Rice

Please note: this book is about writing *shorter non-fiction* material, such as magazine and newspaper articles, pitches, media releases, press statements, essays, reports, academic papers, speeches, etc.

It also deals with the new electronic and computer requirements that are now part of everyday writing.

Our companion volumes, due out shortly, will deal with full-length books, both fiction and non-fiction, including memoir.

For Catherine

(aka Kathleen)

my world

By the same author

Non–fiction

Shattered Vows
The Dragon's Brood
Kirche ohne Priester
The Rathmines Stylebook
Look and Grow Mindful

Fiction

Blood Guilt
The Pompeii Syndrome
La Sindrome di Pompei
Song of Tiananmen Square
I Will Not Serve
Corduroy Boy

In preparation

The Joy of Looking
The Book for the Bully
The Little Roads of Ireland
Red Stag Writing Guides 2-5

Acknowledgements

THIS little book is based on the notes and hand-outs developed over almost 20 years at the Killaloe Hedge-School of Writing. So first I must thank the almost 900 people who have taken part in the workshops, whose constant feedback helped us to develop and refine our thinking. Above all I must thank those professionals who have gone to so much trouble to read, critique, correct and advise on the book's content – in particular, Marie Parker-Jenkins, Professor of Education at the University of Limerick; John Burns, Associate Editor of *The Sunday Times*; Gerard Cunningham, President of the Freelance Branch of the National Union of Journalists; Miriam Donohoe, former News Editor at *The Irish Times*; Aebhric McGibney of the Dublin Chamber of Commerce; Catherine Thorne, Co-Director of the Killaloe Hedge-School of Writing; Maree Murphy, Senior Teacher of English at St. Anne's Community College in Killaloe; Fiona Clark-Echlin, who lectures on writing skills at the University of Limerick; the members of the Killaloe Writers' Group, who have given constant insightful feedback; Joan Lonergan, whose editing eagle eye lets nothing pass. A very special thanks to Jim Walsh, director of Walsh:PR, who has scrutinised the text and whose invaluable PR guidance is on so many pages. And thanks galore to Eugene McDonough, gifted computer guru. Above all, I must acknowledge the late Danny McCarthy, both friend and publisher, whose faith in my work made all the difference. If by any chance I have used insights from other professionals without acknowledgement, I ask pardon. After 38 years of teaching journalism and writing skills – at Rathmines, DIT, and Killaloe – I may well have taken such insights and made them part of my own thinking, now unaware of where they originally came from. I can only say I am both grateful and penitent, and will acknowledge in subsequent editions, if caught out. If this little book achieves its aim, it will be largely thanks to the help and commitment of all these caring people. I can never thank them enough.   *~David Rice*

The KHS motto—

- *Fluency* saves the writer's time
- *Clarity* saves the reader's time
- *Brevity* saves everybody's time

And it all saves money...

Contents

The secret
of effective writing

It ain't whatcha write, it's the way atcha write it
—Jack Kerouac

ALMOST all of us need to write. Some of us have to write newsletters or reports; others need to send a media or press release; some folks want to write for a magazine or newspaper; others just want to write letters to the editor or prepare a speech.

If we're young we might have to write school essays; a bit older, and we might be doing academic papers. Or some of us might just want to write on walls.

Scared to write

The second thing is that many of us are scared to write. We simply don't know how, or think it's too late to learn. And that's because we were badly taught at school.

Most of us thought of writing as a highly special skill to be learnt through sweat and tears (and wallops, if we are old enough to remember those dreary days of walloping).

There is a simple answer to this. Folks in Africa have a saying – if you can speak, you can sing. Well, *we* have a saying – if you can speak, you can write. For *writing is simply frozen speech.* And we can all speak.

Kathy's story

A young woman called Kathy, with a responsible position in a well-known company, came to us for help in writing an important press release. It was about a new product of her company. I sat at my computer and sat her down beside me. 'Tell me,' I said, 'what this is about.'

'A new apparatus for climbing walls,' Kathy began, 'is expected to totally transform the cat-burglary industry throughout the world in the near future. It will be available in sports shops nationwide from next week.

'The apparatus is the result of worldwide development of an invention created in the workshops of Portlaoise Prison...'

Obviously we have changed the content of the above utterance – it certainly wasn't about climbing walls. But the point is this: as Kathy was speaking, I was keying in her actual words. When she had finished I pointed to the screen and said, 'Is that about it?'

'Omigod, that's *exactly* it. Couldn't be clearer.'

'Well, they're your own words.'

Later that day, after a little bit of tightening, we released the text to the media. The following day some of the exact words appeared in two national newspapers, as well as in a news bulletin of the national broadcaster. Kathy has never looked back and is now head of the company's communications and PR.

Speak it

The lesson from this? If you have trouble writing something, speak it out first – quietly, if necessary – even if it means talking to the wall. (Try 'hello wall' if it helps.) Or just inside your head. But *speak* it. And then write down those actual words.

Remember what Voltaire said: 'Writing is the painting of the voice.'

It's that simple. And if you have trouble remembering your words, talk to a recorder – some smart phones can record nowadays.

One other point. Many would-be writers are deterred by the fear that they don't have a wide vocabulary. The answer is simple: Neither do most readers. So if you use words *they* don't know, you've lost them.

Therefore ordinary everyday vocabulary is best – it's how you *combine* those words that makes the difference. (Technical writing of course requires words specific to the profession involved.)

All of this is of course non-fiction, which is what this book is about. Just the day-to-day writing that all of us need. Fiction is a different animal altogether, and we deal with it in our companion volume, *Start That Novel.*

Kinds of non-fiction writing of course vary enormously. Some of the most familiar would include media releases and press statements, report writing, school essays, academic writing, and speech writing. And, if you're a journalist, hard-news writing, feature writing, colour writing, opinion pieces, news reviews, news analysis, sports writing and business writing.

Three formats

There are three basic formats – feature format, hard-news format, and report format. Each requires a considerably different approach.

However there are certain things common to all of them, which can make the difference between interesting, effective writing and dull-as-ditchwater writing.

Remember that dull writing is almost invariably skipped or filed away for 'later' (with later never happening). Which means it might as well never have been written.

The Americans have a number of different formatting styles – *Chicago/Turabian, APA, MLA,* and *Harvard,* which are principally for academic writing. (See page 176.) But for our present purposes we really need only two, and the main difference is in the layout of the paragraphs:

• *Skip-line style:* Each paragraph is separated by a space, but is not indented. This format is normal in business letters, reports and similar documents.

• *Indent style:* Paragraphs are not separated by a skipped line, but the first line of each one is indented (except for the first paragraph). This is the norm for features, hard news, and most books.

Most newspapers and magazines use double quote marks (" "), whereas books use single quotes (' '), as this one does. But best check individual periodicals for which style they use. (In the U.S. even books use double quotes.)

Six keys

What are the keys to effective writing? There are principally six. And they are valid to some degree for almost every category of writing:

Grab the reader's interest;

Hold that interest to the end;

Make them remember it;

Structure what you write;

Develop fluency;

Write with clarity and brevity.

For each of these keys there are a few simple techniques to ensure they are achieved. So here they are, for what they are worth.

Grab the reader's interest

The first sentence can't be written until
the final sentence is written
—Joyce Carol Oates

Y OUR first paragraph (which is always referred to as the *INTRO*) is crucial. *It must grab your reader from the very start.* If not, the reader puts your story down, and moves on to something else. So you might as well never have written it. **(By the way, the word STORY here means anything written for publication – not just once-upon-a-time fairy tales.)**

Burning tyres

French journalists call it 'starting with burning tyres' (*il faut commencer sur les pneus brûlants*) – as a drag racer gets off from a standing start after spinning its tyres till they smoke. Or like a Boeing 737 releasing its brakes, opening the throttles, hurtling down the runway and straight into the sky. Your story must take off that fast. The intro (which Americans call the *lead*) can be a powerful or moving scene, or something that intrigues readers and makes them want to find out more.

In non-fiction, there are a number of ways to achieve this – to grab reader interest. You can start by telling a brief intriguing story (*narrative intro*); or by describing a person or place (*descriptive intro*), and so on. There are many others – quote intro, direct address, summary, question, teaser, humorous anecdote, staccato, contrast, assertion, shock, dramatic statement, etc. A full list of these, with examples, begins on page 22.

The sheep's eye

Laurence of Arabia once told of being invited to a Bedouin tribal feast. There was a complete sheep boiled in the cauldron, fleece, horns and all. As a mark of honour to Lawrence, the tribal chief dipped into the gloop, trawled around until he came up with the sheep's eye, hanging on its trallywaggles, which he solemnly presented to Lawrence, who then had to eat it. Ulp.

That's our model. We need to trawl through the sludge of our notes to find the sheep's eye – the most effective opening or intro. Pick the best, bring it to the top, and present it to the reader as the intro. There may be several possibilities in your notes, so you may have a choice.

Whatever intro you use, *it must really lead into the story.* Otherwise the reader is frustrated because there is no connection. Rather like certain sermons in church, where no one knows what was the point of Father's opening quote from Scripture.

Nut graph

The connection is made by using what is called a *nut graph* (*nut* as in nuts and bolts, *graph* as in paragraph) – i.e., the following paragraph, or even sentence, which locks the intro to what follows, and justifies its use. E.g., intro describes a car being lifted out of the River Shannon at Killaloe. Nut graph says, *This is not an isolated accident. The number of cars falling into the Shannon is growing, and no one really knows why...*

This leads to the point of the article – the mystery of the drowning cars.

The 19 most effective intros

All down the years at the Killaloe Hedge-School we have collected intros from publications all over the world, and we have distilled them down to the 19 most effective ones. Here they are, with examples of each.

1. *Narrative intro*

Everyone loves a story. It immediately catches the interest, and can lead into the main topic of the article. E.g. –

> ON 1 December the peasant Liu Chunshan told his little daughter they would go and visit her auntie. He took the girl on his back. Soon the child was asleep. When no one was in sight he carried her to a well and threw her in. A chill wind was blowing across the wasteland. From the bottom of the well the girl was screaming, 'Ai, Papa, ai Papa.' Liu Chunshan lit a cigarette and smoked while occasionally looking into the well, until the sound of someone struggling down in the waters ceased...
>
> *Nut graph:* Liu Chunshan had been told his wife was pregnant again and a fortune teller had said the new child would be a boy. And he desperately wanted a boy. But why kill his daughter? Couldn't he have a son as well? *No, because China's policy only allowed him one child...*

This leads to the topic of the article – China's one-child policy (now ended, by the way). Note that a hard-news story would prefer a shorter intro than the one above. (See page 127.)

2. *Parable / fable intro*

This differs from factual narrative in that it is a fictional story to illustrate a point. It is one of the most effective of all openings, because everyone perks up to hear a story. E.g. – When they asked Christ who is my neighbour, he didn't give a lecture on neighbourliness. He told a story:

> A certain man went down from Jerusalem to Jericho and fell among thieves...

The nut graph?

> Which now of these three, thinkest thou, was neighbour unto him that fell among the thieves?

Aesop used this technique all the time — *The Boy who Cried Wolf; The Dog in the Manger.* In his case the point was usually so obvious that he didn't even need a nut graph.

3. Shock intro

One of the most powerful openings. If used effectively it can draw the reader right in.

> FOR nine years Don Franco Trombotto, aged 45, had been parish priest of Vilaretto, one of those Italian alpine villages that come alive in summer for the tourists and drowse all winter under their blanket of snow. On 26 January, Don Trombotto hanged himself in the corridor of his parish house, just outside his bedroom door...
>
> *Nut graph:* He had been in love for 20 years but, in the end, not being able to make it official, had killed himself. This is just one example of the tragedy that compulsory celibacy inflicts on Roman Catholic priests around the world...

This leads to the topic of the article: Compulsory celibacy of Roman Catholic priests.

4. Dramatic statement intro

This can be especially effective if it involves the reader.

> ONE of every five smokers who read this will die of cancer or heart disease...

This type of intro hardly needs a nut graph.

5. *Description intro*

This intro can describe a *person, place, thing* or *event.* Examples:

PERSON: JOE Soap has a face like the back of a bus.

Nut graph: But that's not the only ugly thing about him. The creeps who surround him are even worse than his puss...

PLACE: IT was a mountain fortress owned by a wicked baron who killed lots of people. But finally his enemies destroyed that fortress, leaving not one stone upon another.

Nut graph: That's the story of the Berghof, Hitler's hideout on the Obersalzberg, where he...

THING: ONE of China's most splendid treasures must surely be a 2,000-year-old bronze horse unearthed at Wuwei in 1969. Called the Flying Horse, it seems to be galloping so fast that it is stepping on the back of a swallow. The tail stretches flat with the speed; hooves reach forward with incomparable grace on almost horizontal limbs; the head tosses and flares its nostrils and bares its teeth with an exuberance the metal can barely contain.

Nut graph: That sculpture symbolises the Chinese for me – graceful, thoroughbred and proud. Yet in real life it is as if someone had taken that trembling, splendid creature, laid a coarse yoke upon its neck and harnessed it to a wagon sunk to the axles in mud. That wagon is *feudalism.* And the rider that jumped on the horse's back to urge it out is *Marxism...*

EVENT: THE door of the railway carriage slides open with a crash, startling the dozing passengers. *'Passports, bitte!'* snaps the tall, uniformed figure, towering over you in the gloom, lacking only the silver death's-head badge of the SS.

Nut graph: Of course he's just an ordinary German policeman, but that used to be part of the fun of crossing a border by train. It brought back the thrill of the old movies...

6. *General-statement intro*

Caution here: A general-statement intro must lead rapidly to particular detail, otherwise it loses the reader. *Mankind-is-destined-to-suffer* is guaranteed a yawn, although it's often suggested for school essays. It's usually better to start with a particular detail, and work up to the general statement (as shown above in narrative, shock, & description intros, etc). However the nut graph can sometimes save a general-statement intro:

THOUSANDS of Americans travel every year to Ireland, and many are hoping to encounter something connected with James Joyce.

Nut graph: But most miss the best thing of all – Clongowes, that boarding school where he went as a boy, and that figures at the start of *Portrait of the Artist...*

7. Advice intro

Excellent in self-help pieces, especially in popular magazines. Useful too in travel features.

IF you like both your beer and new experiences, and happen to get to Ireland, don't waste your precious moments in the fancy bar of your big-city hotel. Get out across the street to a real pub, where real Irishmen with real cloth caps are contemplating a real man's drink, and sipping at intervals therefrom...

8. Information intro

People like to learn something new. An attractive piece of information can grab the attention and lead into the story. Example:

A MAJOR newspaper estimates that 70 per cent of individuals and almost 100 per cent of couples carry cameras when they travel.

27

> *Nut graph: I* estimate that many of them miss the fun their cameras should give them, because they don't know how to use them properly. Here, briefly, is how...

I'm not sure I'd agree with the above nowadays, since nearly everyone carries a smart phone and can use it very well indeed thank you. Including for photos and selfies. However what it shows about writing skills is still valid.

9. *Summary intro*

This is particularly useful in technical writing. It tells you briefly what the article will contain.

> THERE are three basic controls on a camera: shutter, aperture and focus. Master them and you have mastered photography. Here is how to do it.

The story then develops each item of the initial statement – like development in a Beethoven symphony. Note: Hard-news stories almost always use the summary intro. (See page 127.) E.g. –

> THREE people died early this morning when their car plunged into the River Shannon at Killaloe. The accident took place when...

10. *Direct-address intro*

This is a development of the old Victorian *Gentle Reader*. The best-loved word of all is one's own name. The next best-loved word is *YOU*.

> IMAGINE you have just won a million pounds in the National Lottery. And then you get a letter to say someone else is claiming the money...

11. *Quotation intro*

Quotes lend authority and familiarity. You can piggyback on the eminence of the person quoted –

> 'IN the evening of your life, you will be judged on your love.' These words of St John of the Cross ring as true today as when...

Or you can draw simply on someone's experience. It can be a quote from one who is not eminent or famous –

> 'I was ten when I saw my first executions. My uncle put me up on his shoulders to get a good view. There were six criminals kneeling, each with a gun to the back of his head. I just felt sick, and I didn't want to go to any more things like that... They shot them one after the other and I threw up all over my uncle.'

29

> *Nut graph:* Wu is a Chinese peasant, and he is sharing with me a memory of the Cultural Revolution...

12. *Query intro*

Effective opening, as we are all naturally curious.

> WHAT'S your first emotion on coming across a tragedy, such as a terrible road accident? Compassion? Pity? Care? Sorrow?
>
> None of the above. It's JOY – *I'm glad it's not me!* We may then go on to feel compassion, but first we...

A reader is almost guaranteed to read on, if only to disagree. A query can be particularly effective if it touches on something bothering us –

> CAN arthritis ever be completely cured? If a new drug just on the market is successful, the answer could be Yes...

Caution: Don't leave the question hanging: answer it in the next paragraph or two.

13. Humorous intro

Humour can put reader in a good frame of mind. But beware of cruel humour or too much irony.

> FINDING a good psychiatrist these days is enough to drive you round the bend...

14. Surprise intro

Can be effective, provided the surprise comes quickly (usually in the nut graph).

> YOUNG people nowadays have no sense of duty, no respect for their elders. They just want to laze around, have a good time; and are totally wrapped up in their own selfish interests. God knows what will become of the world when they take over.
>
> *Nut graph:* These are the words of Peter the Hermit, which he spoke in 1095 at the start of the First Crusade. Which shows how little has changed since those days...

This intro can be particularly effective in speech writing, where you have a captive audience. The above intro would make the audience groan in initial boredom, then heave a sigh of relief.

15. Teaser intro

An effective teaser intro functions by triggering curiosity – 'What's this about?'

> LIQUID GOLD. Some say it's addictive. Some say it injures the health. We call each other after it. We compare our loved ones to it. Some of us eat lots of it.

> *Nut graph:* The one thing we can say for certain about honey is that at least it's sweet.

But beware that the headline doesn't give you away. If the headline uses the word *honey*, the teaser won't tease. And headline writers aren't always that bright. Or careful.

16. *Enigma intro*

Something contradictory. Like the teaser, it makes the reader curious. Remember Dickens's opening words of the *Tale of Two Cities* –

> It was the best of times, it was the worst of times, it was the age of wisdom, it was the age of foolishness, it was the epoch of belief, it was the epoch of incredulity, it was the season of Light, it was the season of Darkness...

17. *Staccato intro*

It's rat-tat-tat like a machine gun. Can be effective if used well.

> I came; I saw; I conquered. Caesar wasn't the only one who could truly say that. The new president is probably saying it right now...

18. *Contrast intro*

Readers love contrasts – *then/now; big/small; good/bad; 20 years later; instead.*

> WHEN Joe Soap first started working for newspapers, he had a head of curly black hair. Today he's bald as a coot, pate worn smooth from scratching his head over thousands of news reports he's had to edit over the years.

Another example –

> WHEN Jennie was born prematurely, she looked little more than a foetus. Today, after incredible medical and nursing care, she has become a beautiful 10lb little girl.

19. Assertion intro

This intro is beloved of opinion columnists. It can run the gamut from a convincing point to something outrageous – depending on the columnist. It can be useful for school essays if it's not too smart-ass. Example –

> WHAT I like about dogs is they're so dumb they think I'm fantastic...

Another example –

> ALL poodles should be cooked and eaten in the end. It's the only way they can be made to justify their pampered existence...

Sometimes an outrageous assertion will infuriate readers enough to draw them into the story and make them read it. But be warned – it can get scary if they get mad. The above intro, in a syndicated column in the U.S., almost got this writer lynched.

The hate mail came in huge plastic bags. One letter began, 'Why don't you write about your four-legged mother, you son of a bitch?...' Another one read, 'My poodle is trained to poo on newspapers. Wanna guess which page was picked this morning?...'

Note, by the way, that the above categories are not mutually exclusive. For example, a shock intro can also be a narrative. An advice intro can also be a direct-address intro. Indeed many of them are.

Holding reader interest

Most of our lives are basically mundane and dull,
and it's up to the writer to find ways
to make them interesting
—John Updike

ONCE your opening paragraph has induced someone to start reading, you must hold that person's interest. Otherwise the reader moves to the next article on the page, or closes your book, or puts down your report until 'later'.

The following are ways to hold interest:

- **Careful structure.** A properly structured story is easier to follow than one that meanders. (See page 63 about structuring your story.)

- **Clarity.** If a sentence has to be read twice, it has failed. (See page 49 about achieving clarity.)

- **Short paragraphs.** Indented short paragraphs leave lots of white space on the page, which is easier on the eye and less daunting for a reader. This is known as 'letting air into the text'. We surely appreciate this when we encounter a page or column with no breaks at all. (See page 49 about *brevity*.)

- **Short sentences.** A long one with heaps of dependent clauses puts readers off, especially if they have to read it twice. Or three times... (See page 214 for explanation of dependent clauses.)

- **Use of examples.** Often the words *for instance* are enough to introduce an example. Examples are invaluable in making readable an otherwise dull article or report. They clarify difficult concepts. Examples are in fact mini stories, and everyone loves a story. Indeed we sigh with relief when we encounter one in a dull report.

- **Quotations.** A quote gives a living voice to what you say. It can add authority to your assertion. However too many quotes can irritate readers. They should be relevant and needed.

- **Visual descriptions.** If your writing is graphic, the reader can *see* what you are saying. While this is essential in fiction (*show, don't tell*), even in non-fiction the visual can help. For example, a psychologist about to discuss something could begin – *A patient lately came to me clearly with this very problem. She was trembling, and could not meet my eye...* Carl Jung, in his *Man & His Symbols*, does this brilliantly:

> One of my patients had a very high opinion of himself and was unaware that almost everyone who knew him was irritated by his air of moral superiority. He came to me with a dream in which he had seen a drunken tramp rolling in a ditch...

In other words, the 19 standard intros already outlined – narrative, summary, contrast, surprise, quotation, shock, query, etc – can serve equally well to sustain interest *within* the story. They can be used throughout the text, to move the writing forward, explain concepts, grip and hold attention and relieve tedium.

Humour is particularly invaluable in holding interest. Even some serious writing can be enhanced by a slightly humorous choice of words, or by a humorous example or description. Provided, of course, it's not out of place. Humour can sometimes make a point better than straight argument.

Make them remember it

Make it simple. Make it memorable. Make it inviting to look at. Make it fun to read
—Leo Barnett

IF what you write doesn't go into the reader's memory, you have wasted your time – unless you write exclusively for momentary entertainment.

The ending or conclusion is crucial to this. While the intro's function is to invite readers into the story, the ending serves to put hooks into those readers, so that what you've said remains with them and they cannot shake it off.

Intros as conclusions

The standard intros – narrative, quote, shock, etc – can also be used as conclusions. However their function is completely different here – it is to fasten the point of the story in the reader's memory.

For example, a graphic or harrowing description of an incident at a national border could serve to end a piece about migration. That will be remembered more effectively than any theorising. However it can then serve to recall the theory too.

Return to start

An effective ending can return to the start of the story, reminding readers of the narrative or description that brought them in at the start. We call that 'the snake with its tail in its mouth' (the ancient Egyptian *Ouroborus*). Even Joyce used it in *Finnegans Wake,* where the final sentence is only finished by returning to the very first sentence.

Several of the 19 intros can come together to create an effective ending. Here is the ending to *The Dragon's Brood*, a book about the young people of China, written shortly after the Tiananmen Square massacre:

For the first time it comes home to me that this book is about one-fifth of mankind, not some exotic unknown race in a far distant land. We cannot speak of China's population problem: it is our population problem. China's pollution problem is the planet's problem, and therefore ours. China's sufferings are ours too; her successes are grounds for our joy; her pain must be our pain.

When her young men see visions, they are our visions too. And when those young men and young women die for those visions in a Square far away, we should send not to know for whom the bell tolls....

Here the reader will recognise allusions to two quotations, one from Scripture and one from John Donne. It also conjures up reference to a memorable place – Tiananmen Square.

Unacknowledged quotes

Question: Can you use quotes like the above, *without quote marks (inverted commas),* as we have just done? There is some disagreement about this. I hold that, if a quote is so familiar that it's part of everyday speech, you are paying readers the compliment of expecting them to recognise it. And wouldn't quote marks and bracketed references not simply clutter up and choke the above piece?

Surely a household phrase like *To be or not to be* would look silly if the words *Shakespeare,*

Hamlet, Prince of Denmark, Act Three, Scene One were put in brackets after every such quote. I wouldn't even put quote marks around the phrase.

Or take the example on the previous page – *When her young men see visions,* etc – I feel that that text would be simply choked by quote marks and bracketed references. Even in these not overly religious times, most people would surely know that those young men seeing visions are from Scripture –

> And it shall come to pass afterward, that I will pour out my spirit upon all flesh; and your sons and your daughters shall prophesy, your old men shall dream dreams, your young men shall see visions... *(Joel 2.28)*

And the bell tolling is from John Donne:

> No man is an island,
> Entire of itself.
> Each is a piece of the continent,
> A part of the main.
> If a clod be washed away by the sea,
> Europe is the less.
> As well as if a promontory were.
> As well as if a manor of thine own

42

> Or of thine friend's were.
>
> Each man's death diminishes me,
>
> For I am involved in mankind.
>
> Therefore, send not to know
>
> For whom the bell tolls,
>
> It tolls for thee

A couple of colleagues disagree with me on all of this, maintaining that absolutely everything should be referenced. What do you think, reader?

Fiction endings

(In *fiction,* endings have further functions – to bring a story to a satisfying climax and resolution, and to achieve catharsis; or to put the twist in the tail of an O. Henry short story. These will be dealt with in *Start that Novel* – a companion volume to this one.)

Achieving fluency

No one ever committed suicide while reading
a good book, but many have
when trying to write one
—Robert Byrne

FLUENCY, for our purposes, can be defined as *readiness in the effective use of the written word.* This implies that (1) you select the right word or phrase; and (2) that you select it with as little hesitation as possible.

A total of many hours can be lost within an organization simply by people searching for words when writing memos or reports.

Fluency – short term

Fluency can be *acquired.* There are certain short-term helps. These include—

- Consulting *dictionary* in all cases of uncertainty. This holds both for spelling and meanings.

Use of a *thesaurus,* as an aid to finding the exact word. It must be used with caution, however. (See below.)

• Checking grammar in every uncertainty. (See page 203.)

• Constant use of *stylebook.* (See below.)

It is best always to have a *dictionary* by your side as you write. It allows you to check the meaning of words and their spelling. Or you can simply go to *www.dictionary.com.* Regarding computer spell-check, be careful. For instance It can't tell the difference between *their* and *there.* Or lots else.

Thesaurus & stylebook

A *thesaurus,* which gives lists of words with approximately the same meaning, can be of enormous help, if used rightly. *Roget's Thesaurus* is probably the best known. And there is also *www.thesaurus.com.* A thesaurus is at its best when the word is already at the tip of your tongue, but you cannot think of it. Once you see it in the thesaurus you have a mini *eureka* moment – '*That's* the word I was looking for.'

The wrong way to use a thesaurus is to pick a word at random from the list.

A stylebook, such as *Struck & White* or *The Rathmines Stylebook* (a sister volume to this), takes you beyond grammar into what is accepted style or usage. Constant use of a stylebook will take much hesitation out of writing.

Fluency – long term

All the above are short-term helps towards fluency. Long-term fluency is a different matter, and requires two things – constant practice in writing, and constant daily reading.

Constant practice: This really should include daily writing to create ease with composition. Just as tennis players need constant practice. So you should find something to write about each day, no matter what. If you are writing regularly for your work, that might suffice, but don't bet on it.

Julia Cameron, in *The Artist's Way*, recommends what she calls 'morning pages', where you write something, anything, immediately you wake up (a time when you are most in touch with your unconscious).

You can even write up your dreams, as long as you practise writing. I've been writing up my dreams for years, and I have 47 volumes of them now. If anyone ever got hold of them, they'd be sending for the men in the white coats. Or the Gardai. Not sure which. Actually I am thinking of leaving them in my will to some psychiatric association. Think any would be interested?

Constant reading: It is recommended that we do daily reading for at least half an hour. Preferably lots more. It can be fiction or non-fiction. Quite simply we cannot be effective writers if we are not readers. Constant regular reading has a number of effects:

- It enriches your vocabulary;
- It adds to your range of concepts;
- It brings you new insights;
- Above all, it brings you in constant contact with good writing, and makes you familiar with the way writers use words.

Constant readers find that some sort of gold dust rubs off on them over time, and they find their writing has improved almost without their noticing.

In sum, if you're too busy to read, you're too busy.

Clarity & brevity

Mystification is simple; clarity is
the hardest thing of all
— Julian Barnes

TWO qualities that most make for readability are *clarity* and *brevity*. Yet they are so often ignored, leaving writers wondering why nobody wants to read what they write.

Clarity, for our purposes, can be defined as *the ability of writing to be instantly understood.* This implies that what you write (1) is free from obscurity; (2) free from unnecessary complication; and therefore (3) can be fully grasped *at a first reading*. A total of many hours can by lost by people having to reread, or read several times, material that should have been immediately clear.

Brevity is economy in writing. It can be defined, for our purposes here, *as the use of the exact amount of words required to effectively get across the required information or message.* No more; no fewer.

Here are some of the best ways to achieve clarity in our writing. It sums up much of what has been said already –

- To avoid obscurity, your thoughts must be clear to start with.

- You must have a logical sequence in presenting your thoughts.

- Prepare a written structure, before you write (see page 66).

- Identify your readers, and direct your writing to them.

- Presume your readers are relatively uninformed, and have only moderate interest.

- Avoid abbreviations, initial clusters (e.g., *NCTJ, HIPPA, PSP*), unless familiar (e.g., *GAA, RTE*). Also avoid acronyms (e.g., *Gaat; Ascus)*, unless familiar *(Nato, Nama, Aids)*.

- Use simple vocabulary, matched to your readers.

- Speak out each sentence, if need be, before you write it.

- Use short words, sentences, paragraphs.

- Prefer the concrete to the abstract (See page 205.)

- Avoid dependent clauses where possible. (See page 214.)

- Make your text flow, with phrases such as *this is because...*

- Use examples where possible.

- Put statistics in *sidebars* to avoid clutter (See page 54.)

- Prefer active to passive voice (See page 208.)

- Make the physical presentation attractive and clear.

Let's try to explain some of the above points.

Avoiding obscurity. If your thinking is muddled, your writing will be too. Also, obscure writing is mostly due to wrong ideas of what is required. In particular, people think they have to get into a formal mode and use some sort of formal language. For 'formal' sometimes read 'obscure'.

Some simple techniques make for simple, clear writing: As already said (but worth repeating), if you have trouble expressing an idea, speak out what you want to say, to a colleague, or even alone. Or just inside your head. Then write those actual words. Your words are then sure to be simple: you are unlikely to say, 'In the context of systems deliveries it is envisaged....'

When starting, ask yourself, 'What do I want to say?' Answer in one sentence. Then write that sentence.

Written structure. The best way to achieve this is to make an outline of your story before you begin. (See pages 66-67.)

Logical sequence. Each paragraph should lead naturally into the next, so the reader can follow the argument easily.

Use connecting phrases, like *this is because...* These link to the following paragraph and are known as 'hooks' or 'transition phrases'. There are dozens of such hooks, such as – *as follows; firstly; secondly; and finally; also; on the one hand; however...* Some of these are 'reverse hooks', which link back to the previous paragraph, such as -- *Another instance of this...; for example; in addition; that is to say; in conclusion...*

Some hooks are full sentences, such as – *The result would soon be known.* All such hooks are invaluable in drawing the reader on through the text.

Avoid dependent clauses where possible (See page 214, which explains dependent clauses.) Prefer two separate sentences. If you must use a dependent clause, don't start the sentence with it. If you do, you are putting the reader on hold. (We've just done it here!)

Short words. The shorter the word, the faster it is understood. *Dun & Bradstreet* recommend that 70 per cent of our total words should be of one or two syllables.

Short sentences. If a sentence is long, break it in two. Or in three. That is also the best way to avoid dependent clauses. Few readers can follow sentences with more than two ideas, or containing more than 30 words.

A US study (*Basic News Reporting*, by Ryan and Tankard) found that understanding lessened as sentence length increased. Thus:

Sentence length	*% of readers who understood*
6-8 words –	100%
15	90%
20	75%
25	61%
30	47%

Short paragraphs. *New paragraph every time there is a new idea.* Short indented paragraphs let air into the text. They are easier on the eye, clearer to grasp, and less daunting to the reader. They also help reader to skim. (See page 183 for how to construct a paragraph.) However, even one-sentence paragraphs are acceptable.

In dialogue, one- or two-word paragraphs are often necessary, like –

> 'Do you agree?'
> 'No.'
> 'Neither do I.'

Use sidebars where needed. A *sidebar* is a ruled-off box, separate from the main text. It is a way of corralling off information which, although needed, could clutter up the flow of your story.

Ideal for statistics – readers are assured the stats are there to back up the argument, and can look at them in the sidebar if they want. Most don't bother. (When emailing a sidebar, clearly separate it from the main text and mark it *sidebar.*)

Choose the right word

For your born writer, nothing is so healing as
the realization that he has come
upon the right word
—Catherine Drinker Bowen

YOU may have the most inspired insights, concepts, perceptions but, without the words to communicate them, they are useless to anyone but yourself.

The challenge is to find the *precise* word or words that will exactly express them. English has a wider choice of words than most other languages, since it comes from two sources – French and Anglo-Saxon. The Normans brought in French (derived from Latin) and imposed it on the screaming-and-kicking Anglo-Saxons, whose language was Germanic. Result: *English*, with words from both origins. Which makes it incredibly rich.

Only one word

Yet it's only a slight exaggeration to say that there is only one word that will do, and that you must find it.

There may be a wide choice of words that will *nearly* fit what you want to say, but really only one will say it *exactly*. And you must find it.

You find it thus: you run through your mind, testing all the possible words, until one springs out as the right one. If that fails, your salvation lies in *Roget's Thesaurus* or *www.thesaurus.com*, as explained on page 46. Look up the nearest word to your idea, and then read the other words listed along with it. Usually one will leap out. For in fact you really know what you are looking for, and that is why you recognise it.

What if the required word doesn't leap out? You're in trouble, that's what. However, there are two things that rapidly develop your word sense: constant reading and constant writing practice, as explained on pages 47-48.

Short words

Since English has two primary sources of words, Anglo-Saxon and Latin-derived French, the range of word-choice is vastly greater than most other languages.

But this range means far greater subtlety in word meaning, and a greater need for accurate choice.

All else being equal, when selecting a word prefer one of Anglo-Saxon origin to one from the Latin. Words of Anglo-Saxon are often four-letter words (really!), like *love, hate, kill, work.*

Look at the following list to see how much more powerful they are than the words of Latin origin (which often end in *-ion*). The Anglo-Saxon words are here in italic:

Aversion	*Hate*
Affection	*Love*
Terminate	*Kill*
Mortality	*Death*
Labour	*Work*
Perspiration	*Sweat*
Immorality	*Evil*
Immoral	*Bad*
Masticate	*Chew*
Expeditious	*Fast; quick*
Indolent	*Lazy*
Concupiscence	*Lust*

It's clear from the above that not all Anglo-Saxon words are of four letters, but usually they are at least shorter and more direct. And thus more effective. In other words, outside of technical writing, we need to choose shorter words of whatever origin, rather than longer ones.

The Latin words are often preferred by officialdom and government people because they are longer, more imposing, and vague enough to cloud the meaning. In certain US prisons Death Row is officially called 'the Terminal Wing'.

Word connoisseur

Many years ago a certain leader in the English parliament uttered approximately the following:

> It would not be unperspicacious of us, indeed it would be incumbent on us, to undertake, develop and refine anticipatory and preventive measures to ensure that those who have placed themselves in opposition to our several projects shall in no way be facilitated in whatsoever attempts they may make to subvert and frustrate the efforts that all concerned here are presently making, to accomplish the goals to which we have

hitherto and until now dedicated ourselves in these present circumstances.

The parliamentarian in question was Oliver Cromwell, but he didn't exactly use the above words. What he actually said was –

I tell ye, Sirs, ye must break these men
before they break you !

Well, he's supposed to have said it, anyhow.

Our aim should be to develop a mastery of words – to become a connoisseur of words. So that you can taste the word and know it is just right. Like a chef. Or like Hannibal Lecter – except it wasn't words *he* was into.

Combining words

However, just as a chef is concerned not so much with individual ingredients, as with their combination in a dish, we must be equally concerned with the *combination* of words. Because when the right words are put together the sum is greater than the parts. The words act on each other and can create a completely new thing – which can be explosive.

There are various specialised word combinations and literary devices which further enhance the effect of words on a reader – such as *alliteration* – 'built for burdens and birthing'; 'the Wicked Witch of the West'; *synecdoche* – part for whole – 'the hull sank beneath the waves'; *oxymoron* – 'cruel kindness'; *personification* – 'the moon gazed down'; 'angry clouds'; and *hyperbole* – 'she weighed a ton'.

Adjectives & adverbs

Avoid adjectives and adverbs where possible (See pages 208-209.) They dilute the meaning of nouns and verbs. *Strunk & White*: 'The adjective has not yet been built that can pull a weak or inaccurate noun out of a tight place.'

Just occasionally an adjective justifies its existence. For example, Yeats's '...fumble in a *greasy* till'. But never, *ever*, use two adjectives where one will do.

Other unhelpful words are qualifiers such as *rather*, *quite* and *very*. While there may be occasional need for them, they are often quite useless, very out of place, and rather irritating.

Structure your story

Organisation is what you do before
you do it, so when you do it, it's
not all messed up
—Winnie the Pooh

L ET'S say you're doing an ordinary story for a newspaper – something like an opinion piece, a sports commentary, a fashion piece, a personal experience. The following is a simple way to proceed. (The chapter on page 93 deals with preparing an in-depth story, which is considerably more elaborate.)

First, get together all the notes you have available – memos to yourself, stuff in your files that might be useful, notes you took at that match or fashion show or social function, or notes on a simple gathering of thoughts for an opinion piece or feature article.

Procedure

Here we presume such preparations have been done, and that you now have a set of notes in front of you. The challenge is, of course, to bring together those notes so that they serve the article. Here is an easy way to proceed.

1. Assemble those notes on the desk in front of you. Give each an identifying number or letter (1,2,3... or A,B,C...). If it's a simple opinion piece, put each of your thoughts down on a sheet of paper, and number each.

2. Then range over the ideas to see which way they best fit together. The notes themselves, when seen together, will usually tell you in what order they want to appear.

3. Now do a simple outline or structure of your story. See sample at the end of this chapter (page 66) to see what such a structure looks like. You can handwrite your outline or use the laptop, whichever comes easier. From your notes pick out the main points and note them down, one below the other, in logical sequence, using a brief phrase for each, and putting the identifying number or letter in square brackets [ ]. Then under each heading put the points it gives rise to, again using brief phrases and numbers. The number in square

brackets helps you go straight to that particular note when writing the story.

4. Now search through your notes for the best possible intro (narrative, description, quote, etc), and bring it to the top. Sheep's eye, remember? If your notes don't yield up a good intro, create one there and then.

Write your story based on that outline. If the outline is clear, the story should almost write itself.

Example: On the next page is the outline prepared for the chapter **Breaking into Feature Writing** which appears on page 81.

But note that *your* outlines, since they are just for yourself, need not be as elaborate as the one here on the next page.

Note that the indenting and bullet points help to indicate logical sequence. Note also that the numbers in square brackets [ ] refer to the notes to which the outline refers.

INTRO –Narrative: about how someone broke into print [14]

How to break into print [16]

- Go through one of the journalism schools [4]; or
- Start off as a freelance [5]

That has 2 options: [17]

- Find a periodical that suits your ideas; or
- Suit your ideas to a periodical

Lists of periodicals [22]

- Study chosen periodical
- Study several copies
- Prepare a profile

What profile should contain [9]

- Key names & contact details
- Commissioning editor
- Target readership [18]
- Article length
- Lead time [6]
- Kind of readership [23]
    - ➢ˋAge
    - ➢ Gender
    - ➢ Social class
    - ➢ Education level etc
- Preferred topics
- Attitude [28]
    - ➢ Right wing
    - ➢ Liberal
    - ➢ Feminist etc

Other differences [13]

- Staff written
- Cronies
- Stingy
- Never pay

Becoming a freelance [5]

- What is...?
- Functions of...

National Union of Journalists

- Details
- Benefits of... [16]
- Joining NUJ [14]

Tools of the trade

- No longer just pen & paper
- Need modern tools [10]
- Laptop
- Internet
- Google, Wikipedia ? [3]
- Apps? [2]
- Smart phone
- Camera etc
- Photoshop & Lightroom? [28] [29]
- Question: are all these really needed?

Conclusion: Carpenters have tools. So must you. But main tool is perseverance. [10]

Writing for magazines

In a man-to-man fight, the winner is he who has one more round in his magazine
—Erwin Rommel

JOURNALISM is a cluster of skills, including news gathering and news writing, But also the writing of features. Features are more or less *whatever is not hard-news writing.* (See page 127.) They are the mainstay of magazines, as well as of the features section of newspapers.

There are more than 22,000 publications worldwide looking for features. So there *is* a market for your work – if you can make it professional enough.

Why folks read

People read for many reasons – out of curiosity; for titillation; to know more; to understand better; to keep up with events; to confirm their own beliefs or prejudices; to better themselves; to get help; from interest in people – criminals,

69

celebrities, politicians, royalty – or to learn some skill or science.

Knowing these motivations enables you to produce features to meet those needs.

Kinds of features

There are many kinds of features, such as – personality profiles; interviews; explanations; simplifications (of science, politics, religion, economics, sports); introduction of new ideas; personal experiences; how-to articles; book, film and theatre reviews; memoirs; surveys and polls with their interpretations; horoscopes; quizzes; news backgrounders; news analysis; colour stories.

There is an enormous range of potential subjects, such as – people; health; money; science; business; arts; travel; environment; history; politics; crime; spectator sports; do-it-yourself; religion; hobbies; recreation; sex; animals; plants; home; humour; people watching; world news; local news.

Specialise

Your quickest way to success in feature writing is to specialise. You can then carve out a niche for yourself, and gradually know more than others. Many professional journalists try to have two specialties.

Q. So what can you specialise in?

A. Wherever you have expertise or experience. Obviously your profession or occupation is where your greatest expertise is. *But we need to remember that experience itself is a form of expertise.* Parenting, for instance. Parents are usually experts on child rearing. So we need to take 'expertise' broadly. It can include –

- Whatever you are interested in. A lifelong interest in something means you know more than most. That's a form of expertise;

- What you enthuse about;

- What you have experienced in life – success, failure, tragedy, employment, unemployment, relationships, love, hate, cruelty, generosity, persecution;

- Your hobby;

- Your sport;

- Your area of study; your diploma or degree;

What you care deeply about. If you care

about something, you almost inevitably develop expertise in that area;

• Your voluntary involvement in a cause or charity.

Go to the expert

However you don't write just from your own expertise. That's only a start. You can also piggyback on the expertise of others. In fact one of the most basic skills of the journalist is to know where to find experts, and to get their expertise from them. (See pages 98-99.) Interviewing is a key to this. (See page 119.)

In other words, a journalist can be a sort of midwife, delivering the knowledge from the expert who has it, but who needs help to get that knowledge out.

Having an eye for a topic can be the key to success. Just as engaged couples start noticing furniture shops, journalists are always on the lookout for topics. The lay person sees a derelict site in a busy street and walks on. A journalist wonders why it's that way. There are thousands of topics all around us. Start noticing.

Angles

Also, many general headings have a plethora of angles – we should be aware of them.

The topic of sex, for instance, includes – gynaecological matters; psychology; gender issues; feminism; surveys; romance; marital problems and solutions; health; history; exploitation; the glass ceiling; dress; comparisons (why women drink less than men/ do women pray differently from men?). And so on.

Sources of ideas

We need to be aware of the myriad sources of ideas for features. They can come from anywhere. Some of these sources are often overlooked:

- **Daily & weekly papers**. News items and small ads are a source of ideas that you can develop for features. Local papers in particular.

- **Specialist magazines** provide ideas to rework for general readers. This includes trade publications; underground magazines; minority journals; religious publications, the 'learned journals' aimed at professional groups.

- **The Internet**. Google. Other people's blogs, Facebook entries, even Twitter, and websites galore.

- **Foreign press**. Often these come up with topics that have not yet reached here. If you have a foreign language, you are way ahead.

- **Books.** Read a new book, and write a feature about what it says. Referring to the book, of course. Make the book your story. And indeed it need not be a new book. How about Dickens's take on prisons?

- **Things you observe** – that annoy you, or please you, or intrigue you.

- **Experiences.** Your own, or those that others recount to you.

- **Other people's occupations.** Customs officers, police, family mediators, teachers, train drivers, farmers, street sweepers, street musicians, match makers – all have tales to tell that have never been told.

- **Anniversaries.** Editors love anniversaries and centenaries. Find them by checking Google. Wikipedia's *List of Historical Anniversaries* allows you to pick any date of the year, and recall both events and births.

However, you *do* need to be ahead of the pack, as there's a thing called anniversary fatigue.

• **Spin off from other articles** that you have done. You interview a bore. Well, write him up, but then do a second piece on what makes people boring.

• **Public-relations material.** Governments, interest groups, lobbies, commercial firms, they all churn it out. It can be a great starting point, provided you don't believe the half of it.

They say you should get five articles from every bit of research you do. Rewrite your work to suit various different publications.

Sending by email

Nowadays almost all newspapers and magazines want your feature sent by email. Also, they want it sent without any format, in what's called *plain text,* so they can put their own format on it.

Even so, it is appreciated if editors can also see your fully formatted text, particularly if they want to print it out in hard copy.

So what we suggest is (1) to write and format your feature in the old formal Microsoft Word way, so that both you and the editor can see what it looks like in its final form. (See page 230 for a template that will do this for you.) Then make a PDF version of it (see page 108) and paste it into the email, below your message. Draw a line under it (a few hyphens will do). Then (2) create a *plain text* version, which you simply paste below that. (Go to page 106 to see how to create *plain text*.)

Subject line

An effective *subject line* is crucial. That's the bit that appears on the editor's screen, so it better be good, or the editor will delete before even opening your email. Here's how to create the subject line:

- First click on *Compose*. Obviously you type the editor's email address *in* the first field, which is marked *To.*
- Then click on the field below that, marked *Subject*, and type in the most come-on line you can think of. That's the make-or-break bit.

Pitching

But before doing any of the above, nowadays you are expected to *pitch* the editor *before* sending a feature – in other words, ask if the editor would be interested. This is explained in the next chapter.

Pitching your story

I would advise anyone who aspires to a writing career
that before developing his talent he would be wise
to develop a thick hide
—Harper Lee

W HAT exactly is a *pitch*? Essentially it is an email telling an editor that you have a story that is spot-on for that publication, and offering to write it or send it.

Magazines and newspapers have editors for the various departments, and it is essential to find which editor to pitch to. It is accepted courtesy to use that person's name and email address, rather than just *Dear Editor.*

These names can be found in the guidebooks mentioned on page 83, but those details can quickly go out of date. The magazine's own website often provides the various editors' names and is more likely to be kept up to date.

But sometimes the simplest way is to call the front desk and ask who is editor of a particular department, and what is his or her email.

How to pitch

A good pitch should be *brief and to the point* and should do the following:

- Have a powerful *subject line* so the email actually gets opened. (It's the bit that appears in the email list on the recipient's computer);
- Summarise what you propose;
- Say why it's relevant and timely;
- Say who you are, and why you're the right person to write it;
- State how long it will take to write;
- Mention available illustrations, if any;
- Suggest a deadline for acceptance.

Now, to explain some of the above:

Subject line is of crucial importance – those few words that pop up on the editor's screen, which make her either open the email, or delete it. Take the utmost care to make those words stir enough curiosity to keep that finger away from the delete key. We've said it before, but can't repeat it enough. Remember too that the subject line can often become the headline or title of your piece when published.

Summary: A brief paragraph outlining what your story will be about, mentioning your sources; and pointing out its relevance – such as a coming anniversary; or a specific social problem; information you can provide; or an experience that merits recounting. (As already mentioned, anniversaries are often a soft touch, but everyone else will be going after them too. So get in early.)

Who you are: Then briefly introduce yourself, mention any qualifications, track record or background that would indicate your suitability to write the article.

Illustrations: Mention any pictures or diagrams that are available, their sources, or if you can provide them.

Warning: one editor at a time. Do *not* pitch the same piece to more than one editor at a time. As John Burns of *The Sunday Times* has expressed it to us – 'It's so annoying when you commission something, or are about to commission it, only to find that the freelancer has managed to land it in another publication. One editor at a time; pitch to one publication at a time. Give them a few days, a week, then pitch elsewhere.'

Acceptance deadline: However it's acceptable nowadays to include a deadline for acceptance. This is of course a delicate one, as editors don't like a gun to their heads. But some features editors can be extremely inconsiderate, leaving an urgent pitch or a topical story just sitting there unanswered, until the story is dead.

So it is customary nowadays to include an acceptance deadline, something like – *If I don't hear from you by 23 Jan, I'll take it I'm free to offer the story elsewhere.* Or you could simply say, *Would it be OK if I phoned you in a couple of days to see what you think of the piece?*

(See page 225 for a sample of what a pitch should look like.)

Breaking into
feature writing

Editor: a person employed by a newspaper, whose
business it is to separate the wheat
from the chaff, and to see
that the chaff is printed
—Elbert Hubbard

ONCE upon a time I mailed a packet of five short opinion pieces to the managing editor of one of America's biggest metropolitan newspapers, with the outrageous suggestion that he might like to use me as a regular columnist. I got a reply by return, saying yes, they'd run me every Saturday.

The story is told in full in my novel *Blood Guilt*. Although that's a work of fiction, the sequence about the journalist becoming a syndicated columnist is based on my personal experience.

Yet I don't recommend the procedure, because you need a neck like mine, and you also need to have been a journalist for some years before you attempt the like. But why not work towards it?

You don't have to be a journalist to write features or have them accepted, but it certainly helps. So let's first look at how to get into journalism.

The most effective way is to go through one of Ireland's several schools of journalism. At the time of writing there are nine—

- Dublin Institute of Technology
- Dublin City University
- NUI Galway
- University of Limerick
- Independent Colleges
- Cork Institute of Technology
- College of Management & IT
- Griffith College
- Dublin Business School

These are the recognised gateways to the profession, but some of them can be hard to get into.

So, if you don't manage to get into one of these schools or, if returning to full-time education isn't an option, what can you do? You can start as a freelance. That doesn't mean you have to join the Freelance Branch of the National Union of Journalists, but, again, it certainly helps if you do. (Details on NUJ membership are below in this chapter – pages 88-90.) Apart from that, here are some tips on how to begin. There are chiefly two options – (1) target a periodical, and write what it seems to want; or (2) have something to say, and find a periodical that will let you say it.

Targeting a periodical

Whether you already have something to say, or have nothing particular in mind but just want to write, you first need to find a magazine and study it *in depth* before attempting to write for it. Often simply reading several copies will trigger ideas that you could develop for it.

Most Irish and British publications are listed in the *Writers' Handbook* (Macmillan) or the *Writers' and Artists' Yearbook* (A & C Black), and you'll find thousands of American publications in the annual *Writers' Guide* (Writers' Digest Books). These can be expensive, but they are all available at your local library. In Ireland the *IPA Yearbook* is a godsend.

Profiling a periodical

Prepare a profile of your chosen periodical. You will gain a certain amount of information from the above-mentioned directories but, if you're serious about contributing to a publication, you must also carefully examine several of its *recent* issues. It also helps enormously to go to the magazine's website, which will give you most of what you need to know. You'll need the following information –

• The publisher's address, telephone numbers and email;

• The submission guidelines, which are almost always in the magazine's website;

• The various departments, and the name and email of the commissioning editor for each;

• The target readership – age, gender, social class, education level, etc. You can hardly write a suitable article until you know what kind of readers you will have;

• The kind of articles published in the magazine, and the preferred topics. A study of several back issues will give you a good idea of these, and can trigger new ideas for suitable topics. But beware of suggesting topics that have already been exhaustively dealt with;

• The magazine's attitude. Feminist? Environmentalist? Right wing? Liberal? There's not much point in offering, say, a review of the safest condoms to the Vatican's *Osservatore Romano;*

• The preferred length of articles. Count the words in several articles and make sure your piece matches the average length;

• The *lead time* – i.e., how far in advance of publication must you present your article? Most monthly magazines have a two- or three-month lead time; weekly publications, two weeks to a month. So there is no point in offering a Christmas piece in late November to a monthly magazine;

• The best time to contact the magazine – obviously not close to deadline;

• Preferred method of approach. Most editors nowadays want you to pitch your story first. (See page 77.)

Crucial differences

With 22,000 magazines around the world waiting for your offering, it's understandable that they differ in certain essential matters.

Some are totally staff written, so you are wasting your time even contacting them (unless for a letter to the editor, which some might possibly publish).

Other magazines are open to everyone and welcome and even encourage newcomers. *Ireland's Own* is a brilliant example of this.

Some magazines are open to everyone in theory, but in fact mostly use cronies. You can recognise them by the frequency with which the same bylines appear.

There are certain magazines and newspapers which simply never bother to reply, or will keep your feature unused for so long that it becomes out of date. Get a list of these. How? Just ask around – they are well known in the profession. Some are so stingy that they are not worth writing for.

And some never pay at all.

Regarding stinginess: Freelancers should *never* write for free. That said, don't haggle too much on the first commission. The second commission is the time to argue about the fee if you think it's too stingy. But don't be greedy – newspapers are losing money, cutting budgets, reducing rates. Very few freelancers are making a living; so don't go into this with high expectations.

Also, have a system of checking that your payments are being processed after publication. Most publications have a secretary who processes payments on the day or two after your piece appears. Find out the secretary's name and email. Drop a line if you run into problems – they don't mind hearing from you. They like to keep their books straight so they don't mind you pointing out a missed payment. Saves time and hassle later.

Becoming a freelance

The freelance writer is someone 'who is paid per piece or per word – or *perhaps*!' Robert Benchley never said a truer word. But it should not deter us. OK, it's not easy to break into freelancing, just as it is hard for young barristers to get a first brief, or for new surgeons to find anyone willing to submit to their virgin scalpels. But, as in all walks of life, perseverance pays off.

Suitable topics are all around you. The key is to remember once more the journalist's motto – *to make familiar things new, and new things familiar.*

And one of the most important things that can help is membership of the National Union of Journalists.

National Union of Journalists

You do not need to be a member of the NUJ to break into freelancing. But it helps. The Freelance Branch can help you in 10 different ways –

- Getting paid
- Getting advice
- Copyright
- Press cards
- Training
- Insurance
- Getting work
- Press freedom
- An international voice
- Communication

You can contact the union at *info@nuj.ie* or *info@nuj.org.uk*.

The trouble is getting accepted by the union's Freelance Branch. You normally need to show that you earn half your income from journalism, so it's a bit of a Catch-22. So in theory you simply keep writing until you have enough published to get accepted.

However there are ways around this. If you are trying to establish or re-establish yourself as a full-time journalist, yet do not yet earn half of your income from freelance journalism, and you don't have another full-time job, you can apply online to join as a *temporary member* for three years.

If you do have a full-time job but write on matters of public concern, you can apply for *associate membership*.

If you are over 16 and are studying journalism, public relations, communications, web design or book publishing or, if you are writing for a student magazine, community media, or self-publishing on line or in print, you can apply for *student membership*.

And finally there is *asylum-seeker membership,* for those who are prevented by law from working in their country of residence. They can join for free.

Tools of the trade

If you do persevere, remember that, like surgeon or plumber, you're going to need tools. The tools used to be pen, paper and typewriter – now there are a lot more.

Remember that periodicals no longer accept hard copy (typewritten pages) from freelancers, but insist on electronic copy, simply because there is almost no one to typeset your manuscript. So, if you plan to stick with freelancing, be sure you have the tools.

Laptop, smart phone, email, recorder, are essentials. *Google, Wikipedia,* and apps galore, can be most helpful, if used with caution. Likewise *Facebook* and *Twitter.*

And, if you are including your own pictures with your work, then *Lightroom* and *Photoshop* are equally necessary.

If you are a Luddite who won't touch a laptop, just forget the whole thing. Or get yourself a secretary.

Carpenters have their tools and their skills – these are yours. But the greatest tool of all is perseverance. As we said, anyone can write. But to get published, the key is sticking at it and never giving up.

And nowadays an essential skill is in pitching a story, as already explained above on page 77.

Research & write
an in-depth feature

*Stopping a piece of work just because it's hard... is a
bad idea. Sometimes you have to go on... when
it feels like all you're managing is to
shovel shit from a sitting position*
—Stephen King

THE worth of a feature depends on the research you do prior to writing it. The amount of research varies enormously, according to the kind and depth of your article.

Below are straightforward steps for an in-depth article. But don't let the following details scare you. A lighter piece would require far less detail, but these steps could still serve as a guide.

There are four phases to researching and writing a feature:

One: Background research;
Two: Gathering information from sources;
Three: Writing;
Four: Endgame.

Phase One: Background research

1. Start a file containing everything relevant to what you are writing about. It should contain your preliminary notes and memos, cuttings from papers, photocopies of documents, even your query letter to an editor, and her reply. It should include a rough draft of what you already know, and what you intend to do.

Many freelancers build up files over months and even years on all sorts of topics that they might someday want to write about – news cuttings, references, their own thoughts or epiphanies, etc. This means that a lot is already done before they even start on their research. Cardboard folders are ideal for this. A filing cabinet is a dream come true.

You should try it this way. First, **coarse filing,** involving a simple dump box for notes or cuttings on anything you might find interesting. That can be done over months and years, on lots of topics you may someday want to write about. Later **fine filing**, where every now and then you separate out the items that are useful, file them under topic headings, and dump what you don't need.

Epiphanies

What James Joyce called *epiphanies* can be useful here. An epiphany is some insight that occurs to you out of the blue, but has no immediate relevance to what you are doing. Jot it down in a few words and file it. Maybe years later it will turn out to be a godsend. And it's a way of saving all your bright ideas that would otherwise be forgotten.

There's an example on page 117 of an epiphany this writer jotted down and filed, and then used 20 years later in the intro to the novel, *Blood Guilt* – a connection between a crescent moon and the dorsal fin of a great white shark.

2. Do brief initial reading. Purpose: (1) to get general broad grasp of subject (if you don't already have that); (2) to recognise where your information and understanding gaps are; (3) to get a feel for further reading and research; (4) to know what preliminary questions to ask. Sometimes a general book on the subject, or Google articles, can be a good starting point. But NB. Beware of getting lost in the reading, and failing to make the next step. Also, research must be in proportion to the importance and magnitude of the planned article (and to its possible pay-off – in money or reputation).

3. Prepare a list of preliminary questions that need to be answered for you to write your article. They should at least deal with –

> • The five Ws & H (*what; where; who; when; why;* and *how*). These are simply categories that help you cover all the right questions.

> • Persons relative to your story. Any article becomes more alive if it can be related to some personality. Cf. *Time* magazine's 'personalised news', where founder Henry Luce required that news stories be linked as far as possible to the personalities involved.

> • News hook. Why the article is relevant *right now*. Perhaps the topic is in the news, or soon will be (e.g., an anniversary or current or recent scandal).

4. List your sources. These can include *(a) documents; (b) your own observations or experiments; (c) surveys & questionnaires; (d) people.*

NB. The degree to which you use such sources relates to the depth and seriousness of your article. A light-hearted piece about behaviour in supermarkets might use only observation, whereas an article for an academic journal would use much more.

Documents can include –

- **Your own file contents.**

- **Further references** that you pick up from your reading. Includes key books, found from references and footnotes. Specialist periodicals that carry relevant articles. Libraries contain journals of abstracts, i.e., summaries of relevant articles, plus indications of where to find them. Librarians can direct you in this. Be warned that references grow exponentially, as each one spawns perhaps 10 others – the 'dendritic syndrome', where research gets out of hand, becoming shaped like a tree, where the trunk of initial research ends in dozens of branches and even hundreds of twigs.

- **Almanacs** & specialist guides: e.g., *Encyclopaedia of Associations; Ulrich's*

International Periodical Dictionary; IPA Yearbook.

• **Internet.** Just type your subject into a search engine, and see what comes up. For the moment *Google* is king. *Wikipedia* is great for starting off on something, but be warned that there is dross as well as worthwhile information everywhere.

• **Experiments, observations; surveys & questionnaires.** The topic you are researching will determine the emphasis here. Research in pure science might stress experiments; in the social sciences, you might draw more on surveys, or participant observation.

• **People & other sources.** At this point you list the names of personal sources – those who can help you with information or expertise. These are either experts or persons with a relevant experience. A rough rule of thumb is three to five sources per 1,000 words. Five for a serious piece; three for a lighter piece. Sources can include –

✓ Professional organizations;

- ✓ Voluntary organizations;

- ✓ Interest groups; pressure groups; lobbies;

- ✓ Central- & local-government officials;

- ✓ Staff of trade magazines – those in smaller magazines are often ready to talk, or to recommend others;

- ✓ Commercial organizations, especially their PR departments;

- ✓ Academia – the information offices of universities will gladly put you in touch with their resident expert in a given area;

- ✓ Librarians, often the best of all guides;

- ✓ Internet. There are websites dedicated to finding you the expert you need. They include ProfNet *(www.profnet.com)* and Newswise *(www.newswise.com).*

- ✓ Citation engines (See page 177.)

Note that one source can often provide several more. List them all, with phone numbers. Later you can decide which to use, selecting the most professional or most knowledgeable.

Phase Two:
Gathering information from sources

• **List your source categories**, such as pro and anti; experts; perpetrators; victims, etc. In a story about *metal-detector abuse*, categories could be – treasure hunters; government officials; police; technical experts; foreign antique dealers; fences, and so on.

•**Prepare your list of questions**, to be put to your sources. Different questions for different sources, and all aimed at eliciting the information or expertise your article needs.

• **Using your sources** involves telephoning, emailing or going to meet them. Sometimes telephoning or email is sufficient, but face-to-face interviews often yield the best information, simply because your presence brings out the best in the person. Usually.

The first contacts should be – those with the best knowledge; those likeliest to be helpful; and sometimes those who will be hardest to get (because it may take longer to get them). Go to the best experts you can reach, at the beginning. Then work your way down.

When phoning, have your first words rehearsed, and have your questions written out beside you, so there is no hesitation. Keep questions brief, and to a minimum.

Face-to-face interviews have a chapter all to themselves on page 119. They are often crucial to an effective in-depth feature. It might be a good idea to turn to that chapter now, before continuing here.

Phase Three: Writing the story

At a certain point, stop researching and start writing. At what point? When the questions still unasked are mere minor details that can be checked later. Otherwise we might never start. Proceed as follows:

1. Winnow your material, cutting out what is not relevant. Take the relevant material from your project file and place it in a new file marked *manuscript file*.

2. Sort that material into categories. E.g., in *Metal-Detector* article, categories might be –

- Details on those who use them;
- What the treasure hunters themselves say;

- Opinions for;

- Opinions against;

- Official government views, statements;

- Police views, comments;

- Comparisons from abroad;

- Evidence of site destruction;

- Evidence from overseas;

- Expert opinions;

- What remedies?

- Existing legislation;

- Proposed legislation;

- Possible intros (quote; narrative; etc);

- Possible endings.

Within each category *there may be several items.*

3. Give each *item* a number in square brackets, like this [ ]. Note: number the *item*, not the category. This will let you go straight to that item when writing the story.

4. Study the categories, *until they form a pattern.* An outline of your article will begin to grow in your mind, as you go back and forward through the categories. As the outline grows, write it down, putting the item number beside it. It will look something like this:

1. Quote intro: Ireland is being harmed by treasure hunters, says Government spokesperson. [21]

2. Why? Because --

- *sites are being wrecked by digging, e.g.,*
    - ➤ *Clonmacnoise [17]*
    - ➤ *Skellig Michael [32]*
- *treasures are being sold overseas.*
    - ➤ *Three examples of this [5; 41; 16]*
    - ➤ *Quote from US antique dealer [27]*

3. Who are these treasure hunters? There are two kinds: [12]

- *Amateur, just for fun*
- *Professionals, for profit*

4. What can be done about it? [29]

And so on. But remember, *the outline should be written down.*

5. Start writing, letting the outline guide you. When you come to *Clonmacnoise*, dig out item 17 from your file, and write that into your story. Then go to 32, and write about *Skellig Michael*. Continue until story is complete.

6. Go back up to your intro, to see if it is powerful enough. If not, replace it with a more effective one (one of the 19 intros given from page 21 on – *narrative, shock, quote*, or whatever suits).

7. Do the same with your conclusion, again drawing on the 19 intros, which function equally well in a conclusion, making memorable what you have written.

(At this point some writers insert what are called *sideheads*. These are a couple of words in bold type, placed between certain paragraphs to introduce a new idea or direction, and also to break the monotony of a page. Other writers leave it to the sub-editor to put them in. They are used throughout this book – for example, '**All five senses**', on page 109.

8. Sleep on it. That is, if your deadline allows it. You will always find things that need changing next morning.

Phase Four: Endgame

We already said that writing is just frozen speech. And that's true, but that doesn't mean it doesn't need editing. So, next day, look at your article again. Take off your writer's hat, put on your editor's hat and take out your scalpel. (Remember that old saying of editors – *Kill your darlings!*)

1. Check the following:

- Spelling & grammar (spell-check is rarely enough);
- Accuracy (names; places; quotes, etc);
- Attribution (have you attributed information, quotes or expert views to your sources?);
- Word count;
- Excessive words;
- Sloppy sentences;
- Too many dependent clauses (see page 214);
- Sloppy logic;
- Repetitions;
- Flow (does the text flow easily, or could it be improved?).

Note: What follows is the traditional way to present a feature, with headline, indented paragraphs, etc. Even though it is no longer what editors want (see *plain text* on next page), we recommend you still do it to get a proper feel for what you have written. (Then you can reduce it to that loathsome *plain text* that editors nowadays insist on.) So –

1. Write a succinct *working headline* in 24pt bold, and put it at the top.

2. Write a brief *standfirst* that sums the story up in one sentence. Put it in 12pt italics *above* the headline.

3. **After the last paragraph**, put the word ENDS, followed by one sentence in bold type giving brief relevant details about yourself as author. (See pages 227-230 for an example of this.

Final plain-text format: In theory your story now has all the professional touches – set in 12pt Times New Roman; paragraphs indented, except the first; first word in caps; no space between paragraphs.

But none of that is required any more. In fact it's a nuisance, as editors have to get rid of all your formatting, and then download your text into their own template which produces the format they need.

So – now you must reduce the whole thing to PLAIN TEXT –, no font specifications – *just the bare words*. As for paragraph breaks, as long as you have already hit *return* for each new paragraph, that's OK. So how to get plain text? Here's how –

- When your piece is finished, click on *File,* then on *Save as*;

- Two fields appear. The bottom one reads, *Save as type.* At the right, you will find a **V**;

- Click on the **V** to get a drop-down menu. Scroll down until you get to *Plain text (*.txt)*;

- Click on that;

- Then click on *Save;*

- Highlight the whole thing *(Home,* then *Select,* then *Select all)*;

- Hit *Ctrl-C* to copy it;

- Go to the introductory email that you have written to the commissioning editor. (If you haven't written it, do it now.);

- Click below your message, and hit *Ctrl-V* to paste your plain-text story in.

- Click on *Send.*

As already said, you can if you wish also include the fully formatted version, simply to show what the finished story looks like. Simply add it to the email, preferably above the plain text, separated by a row of hyphens.

There is a model of full-feature format on page 227, and a template to create it on page 230. As we said, although no longer necessary, it can be a help to write it in that format anyhow, to get a feel for the final result, and to give the editor a feel for it. *Provided of course you then reduce it to plain text, as shown above.*

If you do decide to include a full-feature format, you should first copy it, then convert the copy to PDF so it remains unchanged in the email. Simply go to *file/print/printer* – then drop down to *Microsoft-to-PDF*. A field called *File name* will appear. Type in your name for the piece. Then scroll up the left-hand column and click on the word *Desktop*. Click on *Save.*

Find that icon on your desktop, open it, click on *Home/Select/Select all*, copy it *(Ctl-C)*, go to your email and paste it in *(Ctl-V)*. That's it.

The writer as observer

Every secret of a writer's soul, every experience
of his life, every quality of his mind,
is written large in his works
—Virginia Woolf

SAINT Thomas Aquinas said that memory is coextensive with interest. So is observation: if you are setting up house, you start noticing furniture shops. Since a good writer is concerned with everything, he or she must notice everything. It comes with practice and growing awareness.

All five senses

According to Carl Jung there are only two ways we can gather information – (1) from *intuition* or (2) from our *five senses*. (Then *intellect* classifies the information, and our *feelings* evaluate it.)

So, if our writing is to be powerful and three dimensional, the observations on which it is based – our noticing – must use *all five senses* as much as possible.

So the only way we get knowledge (apart from intuition) is through those five senses – Hearing, seeing, touching, tasting, sniffing.

Dogs prefer sniffing; we mostly prefer looking. But the best way we can convey an impression (fiction or non-fiction) is by getting to the reader's five senses.

So a writer needs to notice everything, using all of those five senses:

Sight. We need to see things that others don't notice. How light filters through beech leaves and lights them up so that they glow. Or how at night a pinpoint of light can be seen for miles. Shakespeare noticed that: *How far that little candle throws its beams....* Especially we should notice colours and their subtleties – they say there are eleven million colours visible to the human eye. The circles on a peacock butterfly's wings. Or a bee moving into a rose. Or body language, especially when someone is embarrassed, angry, contented or smug. Or faces in the street – the contented ones, the angry ones, the anxious ones. We can learn to tell the difference.

Hearing. Wind in the trees, exciting or menacing. The growl of a Mazda MX-5 exhaust. The myriad songs of a thrush or a blackbird. The 13 songs of the lark – the Chinese say it has that many. The beat of a swan's wings: Yeats observed that at Coole – *The bell-beat of their wings.* A peal of thunder, too near to be comfortable. The crack of a gun. The whisper from an airliner far above.

Smell. New-mown grass. Dentist's surgery. Old muddy football boots. Unwashed armpits. Freshly sawn wood. Damp wool. That girl's Chanel No.5. A just-bathed baby. A wet cocker spaniel. TCP on your finger. NB. Smell is the most evocative of all the five senses and easily conjures up memories. Psychologists tell us that smell relates to some primitive part of the brain, so maybe that's why.

Taste. Red wine on the palate. Sea water in mouth and nose as you plunge into the Atlantic at Lahinch. That ghastly medicine from childhood. Hot buttered toast. That last luscious chocolate from the box at Christmas that had been left for somebody else. A T-bone steak done to a T.

Touch. The feel of varnished wood. The quivering warmth of a puppy. Bare feet on damp grass. Same bare feet walking into dog shit, and it creaming up between the toes. Silk between the fingers. Velvet when caressed.

NB. The sense of touch can be aroused even through sight or hearing – e.g., the *texture* of a damp pavement or of gleaming velvet can evoke the sense of touch, even if it is only seen with the eyes. Remember Rupert Brooke's *Wet roofs beneath the lamplight...* ? As for hearing, how about chalk screeching wrong way across a blackboard? Or someone filing his nails?

Observation

The ability to observe and notice things actually can grow in a writer. Indeed it must do so. However, observation by all five senses is only half the gift.

The other half is to be able to weave those sensual observations into our writing. If our writing is to be really alive it must continually be touching all five senses of the reader.

It is surprising how such evocation of senses can be achieved. E.g., 'His face looked as if he had just sucked a lemon.' Or 'His voice sounded

112

like clotted cream.' Both of those evoke, not just sight and hearing, but taste and touch.

Feelings

There is one further source for a writer, besides intuition and the five senses. It is the writer's own inner feelings – sadness, angst, joy, hate. These can enrich our writing, even in non-fiction.

For instance, our feelings on describing a city after a tsunami or a bombing raid.

More than 30 years ago this writer reported on the eruption of Mount St. Helens, in the U.S. Pacific Northwest. After flying in and around the raging mountain, and witnessing the horror of its devastation and slaughter, I found myself expressing hate for it as if it were an evil living thing. For that's how I felt. My final sentence described the mountain as 'vomiting its filthy burden at the sky'.

Colour writing

Writing that uses the five senses, descriptions and feelings, as outlined above, is often referred to as *colour writing.* It can be astonishingly effective when done with skill, and can add much to a writer's reputation.

Write with wonder

Those who contemplate the beauty of the earth
find reserves of strength that will endure
as long as life lasts
—Rachel Carson

THE world around us is magic, but few of us have learnt to look. Especially to wonder at it. *But wonder is one of the secrets of creative writing (indeed of creative living).* How about the following:

The sky as a gigantic canvas where God or nature (whichever you're into) paints her abstract creations of blue and white and crimson and gold, then wipes them out and starts all over again. She rests only at night, yielding then to the stars. I am not trying to be poetic – quite literally, the sky above us is the greatest of all spectacles that the human eye can behold. We simply don't notice it because it's always there.

Light. When did you last notice light – dancing on a lake; slanting through forest mist; sparkling in a child's eye; chasing down a mountainside as the clouds race overhead; driving through a girl's fair hair to create a rim light like Marilyn Munroe?

Self – the miracle that we ourselves are – the lines on our hand, etched into the palm before we were born; our camera called the eye. The incredible organism that is oneself – an organism that navigates by vibrations of light and communicates by vibrations of air; that can reproduce itself; and, above all, that can become aware of itself and ponder its existence. When did we last wonder at ourselves?

Shapes – trees, with trunks rising into branches, smaller branches, and finally thousands of twigs. Same shape as the Shannon – main trunk the great river; fed by tributaries; then little feeder streams. Lightning the same shape. The tree-shape of our bloodstream – arteries; veins; smaller veins, capillaries. Nervous system the same, from the spinal cord to the brachial plexus to the median nerve all the way to the nerve ends at our finger tips.

It's called the *dendritic* shape (from *dendron*, Greek for a tree), and it's in all of nature. Even our family tree is that shape. And our body too: the trunk (we actually call it that), limbs (our branches), fingers (our twigs).

Connections between things – being creative as a writer (and as a thinker) means seeing connections between things that no one else has noticed. It gives us similes and metaphors. E.g. –

His voice would make you think of whipped cream.

Her screech sounded like shattering glass.

Clouds like cottage loaves, round on top, flat underneath.

A crescent moon coming up out of scudding cloud, like the dorsal fin of a great white shark.

Look –

In expressing such connections, *metaphors* are more powerful than *similes*. A simile states that one thing is *like* another; a metaphor *identifies* them. For example:

- *Simile:* The spike of a crescent moon came up out of the line of scudding cloud above Newry. As it sliced through the cloud it was like the dorsal fin of a great white shark.

- *Metaphor:* The spike of a crescent moon came up out of the line of scudding cloud above Newry. As it sliced through the cloud it was the dorsal fin of a great white shark.

There is only one word omitted in the metaphor, but it makes for a much more powerful effect.

Incidentally, philosopher Arthur Koestler once said that creativity consists of seeing those connections that no one ever noticed before — bringing the concepts of two totally different things together for the very first time. Moon and shark, for instance.

It's actually the source of many inventions: *Velcro*, for example. In 1941 a Swiss scientist was walking through a meadow when he noticed his doggie covered with sticky burrs. Under a microscope he discovered that the burrs were covered in tiny hooks. The thought occurred: why not use such tiny hooks instead of buttons? So – buttons and burrs, linked for the first time.

The interview as a source

I always start writing with
a clean piece of paper
and a dirty mind
—Patrick Dennis

AMONG the building blocks of research for writing – which include observation, reading, experimentation, experience – the *interview* ranks high. It is an effective way of acquiring knowledge that you cannot get from your own observation, reading or experience. It's a way to piggyback on another person's knowledge and experience.

Detail

The interview can help you with both fiction and non-fiction. It answers *what, when, where, who, why and how.* (In fiction it can bring you realistic detail you would not otherwise acquire.)

An interview can be done face to face, by telephone, by *Skype*, *What's App* or *FaceTime*, but in all cases preparedness is the key. The face-to-face interview is the most effective, as you can see ambiance and body language. However the telephone interview can be handier and quicker.

There are two broad categories of interview:

- **Informational / scientific**—i.e., seeking someone's knowledge or expertise;
- **Personal**—i.e., seeking details about someone's life, personal experience, etc. This can often be a personality profile.

Interviews can be with celebrities or with ordinary folk (who are usually far more interesting). With celebrities you are mostly seeking hitherto unknown personal information; with non-celebrities you are seeking their experience, knowledge, expertise, wisdom, memories, outlook or opinion.

Before the interview

Preliminary or background research is essential. For a scientific interview, you must at least know enough to ask pertinent and intelligent questions. Preliminary research of the subject ensures this. For a personality interview you should know all you can about interviewee, so you don't ask about things already well known. A celebrity can turn nasty if you ask something that everyone already knows.

• Prepare a set of about 10 questions. When relevant, they can be based on the five Ws and H (*what, when, where, who, why & how*). Write the key-word of each question in large type, one below the other. Keep them beside you during the interview, so you can glance at the list without fumbling. With a telephone or Skype interview, prepare and rehearse your opening words.

• Try to arrange the interview in the person's home or office, rather than in a hotel lounge – the ambiance gives you clues to the person.

Doing the interview

• Arrive early, to get time to look around and absorb the atmosphere.

• Sit at right angles to interviewee. That eliminates staring into the face, but allows eye contact whenever either person wants.

• Try to take notes, using recorder only as a back-up. Also take notes on non-verbal things such as body language. A recorder won't catch those.

• Do have frequent eye content, especially when putting questions.

• The more the interviewee talks, the less you should. At times nods and encouraging murmurs are all you will need. As the Scripture puts it in a rather different contest:

> He must become greater;
> I must become less —*John, 3.30*

• Do not accept an alcoholic drink. Even one will blunt your keen questioning, and may cause you to miss certain nuances.

• For personality-profile interviews, start with easy questions (about background, etc), and work up to the difficult ones. That puts the interviewee at ease, as well as yourself.

• Exception to the above: If you are aware that the interviewee is going to kick for touch or give you a snow job, go for the jugular with your very first question.

• Don't stick rigidly to your 10 questions. In personality interviews, if the interviewee goes off at a tangent, go along with it if it leads to interesting revelations. Whereas in informational or scientific interviews, you usually require only specific answers to queries, so stick to those topics. This is especially true if time is short (as in radio interviews or on the telephone).

• Ask for examples – they leads to narratives, which enrich your interview.

• For a personality-profile interview, use leading questions. This sort of thing, *but tailored to the particular interviewee*:

✓ What was your first job?

✓ When did you last cry?

✓ Tell me about your first love.

✓ What gave you the most joy/sorrow last year? Or in your lifetime?

✓ Your desert-island choice of books, CDs or DVDs?

✓ Your most vivid memory from childhood?

✓ Who would you like in a hospital bed beside you?

Recorders? Take written notes as best you can. *Always.* (If you have shorthand, kneel down and thank God.) But if possible also use a small, unobtrusive recorder (preferably voice-activated). Some smart phones can do, at a pinch, but many have limited capacity.

Start the questions without the recorder. Then lift out the recorder, asking, 'Mind if I use this?' But remember, a two-hour interview means two more hours playing it later (usually far more).

Actually even if you have shorthand or can take adequate accurate notes, it's good to have a recorder there, just as a back-up in case there is disagreement later, or even legal problems.

Ending the interview

Always end with, 'Is there anything else you would like me to ask you?' Or 'Is there anything we've forgotten?' That often brings the best bits.

Before you leave, make sure you have contact number and email address, as you often will need to check a detail later.

After the interview

Write up your notes before they grow cold. Try to use actual quotes from interview – the exact words.

Sandwich direct quotes between indirect ones. (Indirect quotes are not actual words of interviewee, but things like *She told me that she always...*)

Also try to include your observations of the scene, of the ambiance, atmosphere and body language (where appropriate).

NB. *Be wary of showing your write-up to the interviewee – who will often want to change everything.* If asked, try to weasel out of it by saying that your editor wouldn't wear it.

Note: In personality interviews, there can be certain no-go areas. Unless otherwise agreed, and *unless there is a real reason why you should*, do not ask about – sexual orientation, sex experience, income, acreage, herd size, religious affiliation, political affiliation, certain family relationships, marital status, cohabitational status, education level. Unless of course the interviewee volunteers it.

It's obvious why. Or even if it's not, just don't. Unless you have a jolly good reason.

Of course the times they are changing, and this advice may well be out of date by the time this gets printed.

The hard-news story

In a fascist shift, reporters start to face more and more harassment, and they have to be more and more courageous simply in order to do their jobs
—Naomi Wolf

THE hard-news story is the bread-and-butter of news reporters, but we can all use the format to our benefit.

It is, or should be, the basis of most media releases, bulletins, notices and announcements. It can also be the basis of many ordinary letters.

The hard-news story simply gives straightforward news – information about something that has happened or will shortly happen. E.g., reporting a serious accident; a new business venture; a new invention; a death; a planned sale of work; an engagement.

The five Ws & H

The hard-news story normally should answer six questions – *What? When? Where? Who? Why?*

How? (the five Ws & H). There is a standard structure to the hard-news story:

The first paragraph (*intro*) states the essence of the news (the key fact or 'news point'). E.g.,

- *Two men died early this morning when their car...'* or

- A *sale of work will take place Friday (15 June) in ...*

Usually answers *what, when* and *where*.

The second paragraph (called the *catch-all*) gives further essential details. Usually gives more of the five *W*s. It should also include *attribution* if required – i.e., stating the source of the information.

(If there is a way to tie in the reader, it can be done in the next paragraph. E.g., *Motorists are regularly warned of the danger of this part of the highway, according to a police spokesperson.*)

Then follows the **transition to detail**, where required. (E.g., *Witness said the accident occurred when...*)

The rest of the piece simply **develops the story**, with further detail. It serves to amplify the intro, as well as explaining and justifying it.

The details are then presented in **descending order of importance**, so the story dwindles to the least-important detail at the end. (E.g., *The late Mr Smith had been a leading member of the Gourmet Club...*) Who gives a toss? This allows the editor to delete from the end upwards, when space is scarce, and also allows the reader to skim – i.e., to get the main story in the first few paragraphs.

It is clear therefore that the hard-news story is utterly different from the standard feature format with its 19 grab-the-reader intros. It uses only the *summary* intro, and goes out not with a bang but a whimper – fading to nothing at the end.

This format is known as *the inverted pyramid* – wide at the top *(= important)* and getting narrower all the way down *(= less important),* as in the diagram on page 131.

The diamond

However sometimes a reporter or news editor will introduce one of the 19 intros *before* the hard-news item, to lighten the effect or draw the reader in. Something like this:

> THE scene was like something from a Hollywood B movie, with all the drama of spies in a posh Moscow restaurant, and a bad guy in a false moustache, tinted glasses and a panama hat.
>
> But this was no movie, as was clear when political activist Yevgeny Zhilin was suddenly shot dead by the man in the panama hat, who then ran out to the waiting Range Rover...

This format, which can be effective if not overused in news bulletins, is referred to as a *diamond*, for the obvious reason that the widest part – the actual news item – is a paragraph or two down from the top – and the rest is in inverted-pyramid shape, as in the diagram opposite. So the whole shape is like a diamond.

Sperm format

There is also the s*perm* or *tadpole* format, where the intro (head) contains enough information for the story to survive even if the rest is cut off – as happens to those poor little critters.

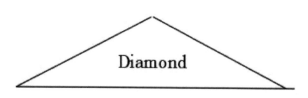

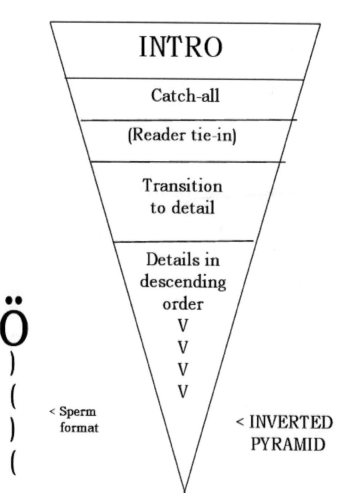

Diamond

INTRO

Catch-all

(Reader tie-in)

Transition
to detail

Details in
descending
order
V
V
V
V

Ö
)
(
)
(

< Sperm
format

< INVERTED
PYRAMID

Its main function is to allow the intro to be presented in a front-page summary of news, which then refers the reader to an inside page where the full story appears, using the same intro. *The Irish Times* is an excellent example of this.

Clarity & simplicity

Hard-news stories should avoid dependent clauses (page 214), technical jargon, unfamiliar words, foreign words, questions, or initial clusters such as NKVD or BRM, unless utterly familiar to readers.

It should also avoid what are called *portmanteau intros* – e.g., 'The Taoiseach today made an important announcement regarding Northern Ireland.'

Just tell us what he said.

Preparing a media release

There's villainous news abroad
—Shakespeare

A MEDIA *release* is a statement issued to the news media to announce something newsworthy (or thought to be so, for lots are not). It's also called a *press release, news release,* or *press statement.* There are three basic kinds: (1) A news item to be published *as is*; (2) material to be used as backgrounder; (3) feature-type piece aimed at publication.

Passing the gatekeeper

We are concerned here with (1), which is most frequently required. Aim is to get it past the editor/gatekeeper, and into print as news. Best achieved by making it a standard hard-news story, so it doesn't have to be rewritten in the newsroom. If it needs editing or rewriting, it simply won't go in. Nowadays almost all media releases are sent by email. Points to remember:

- The *subject line* (the bit that appears in the email list on the recipient's computer, and that you write in the *Subject* field after clicking on *compose*) should be as come-on as possible, to keep that hovering finger off the delete key.

- Your release must be short, succinct and precise. Best around 250 to 500 words – never more than 800. Best in four or five paragraphs. And clear and catchy as possible.

- Follow the rules of hard-news writing – the five Ws & H *(What, where, when, who, why & how);* the inverted pyramid (intro; catch-all; reader tie-in; transition to details; details – all in descending order of importance; *attribution where necessary*; brevity.

- The intro must present absolute essence of story – no more, no less.

- Your release should be in the body of the email, *not sent as an attachment.* Editors are scared of attachments, for security reasons.

- Keep intro as brief as possible, with two or three of the Ws (balance in catch-all). The following are examples of required intro word-limits for various papers –

> The Irish Times – 28
> Associated Press – 32
> Daily Mirror – 20
> The Sunday Times – 30-40
>> – *says former editor Harold Evans*

Not that the journalists seem to bother much about such limits nowadays. However *we* had better observe them. (Book chapters can have longer intros, but that's another story, dealt with in our companion volume, *The Non-Fiction Book*).

Some guidelines:

• Do not indent intro, and put the first word in caps.

• Indent all other paragraphs.

• No space between paragraphs – the indents are sufficient.

• Keep paragraphs as brief as possible.

• Eliminate *non-essential* information, such as – at which venue the announcement was made; irrelevant quotes (CEO *Jonathan Bumble expressed his delight that...*); who attended the reception (unless the story is about the reception itself, or the attendee's name is important). Of course if Mr Bumble is the top boss and wants his delight noted, don't lose your job over it. Remember, your client is your first gatekeeper.

• When in doubt as to format, look at a brief news story in a reputable newspaper, and take that as a model. Do this regularly. Or take a look at the model on page 222.

• At the end of the text, put the word ENDS in caps, centred.

• Below that put, in bold, **For further information, contact...**, and give your name, phone number and email (if different from the one being used).

• At the top put a clear and simple headline, in 24pt bold Times New Roman.

• At the beginning of the first par, put what is known as the dateline. It goes like this: *Dublin, 23 June, 2019.* It should be part of the paragraph, not separate.

- Make sure the email has a *signature line* – similar to a company letter head, but placed at the bottom. It should have all necessary details, including address and phone numbers.

- It is recommended also to include at this point what's called a 'boilerplate' – i.e., a brief, succinct description of the company or organization. You can head it *Note to editors*.

- It's often a good idea to include a *standfirst* – a brief one-sentence or bullet-pointed summary at the very top. Put it in bold, in narrower margins, with the words **IN BRIEF** at the start. (See example on page 222.)

- Use 12pt Times New Roman (<- like this) for body of story. Never *ever* use a sans-serif face (that looks like this) such as Ariel or Calibri. They are tiring on the eyes and editors detest them.

- Set everything left-aligned, with the right side of the text ragged (like the paragraph above this one). To do this just highlight the text and click on ▤ at the top of the screen.

• Many editors ask that you repeat the whole thing in *plain text* below the release, to allow editors to put their own format on the text if they plan to print it. (Creating plain text is explained on pages 106-108).

• If you plan to include a picture, note what we said about attachments. Editors prefer that you send the picture direct to the paper's Picture Desk, with a caption embedded. If you do so, note that in the release.

Report writing

You don't actually have to write anything until you've
thought it out. This is an enormous relief,
and you can sit there searching
for the point
—Marie de Nervaud

THE procedure for researching and writing a formal report is roughly similar to that for an in-depth feature. (See page 93.) But there are certain essential differences:

1. A report is usually commissioned;
2. It is for a particular person or group;
3. It can be considerably longer;
4. It must meet laid-down criteria;
5. There is usually a deadline;
6. There is a standard structure to a formal report;
7. There is a place for technical language, particularly if the report is aimed at people within an organization or profession;

8. There is little place for the 19 standard intros;

9. An utterly logical sequence is required;

10. Headings and paragraphs are numbered in one of several standard formal ways (*1*; *1.2*; *1.2.2*; etc)

However none of this means that the report has to be dull. And so many reports *are* dull, since written perhaps by experts in their field, but who are far from experts in writing.

The same need for fluency, clarity and brevity – as outlined in this book – are paramount to good report writing. Indeed, the principal reason reports have an *executive summary* is that it's often the only bit the executive reads – or is even able to read – while the rest gathers dust on an upper shelf in a CYA (cover-your-ass) capacity. Usually because it's so dreary.

Formal report structure

Below are listed the usual components of a formal report, although not all reports will require all of what follows. Beneath each heading are listed the items, some or all of which are contained in that section:

Title page

- Title
- Date
- Author's name
- Reference number if required
- List of those to whom the report is to be circulated
- Warnings like *Confidential* if required

Terms of reference

- Aims, objectives and scope of the report;
- Roles and responsibilities of those involved;
- Resources available – financial, planning, and structural;
- Intended readership;
- Time frame – when report is to be completed.

> *(Note: terms of reference are sometimes placed in the Introduction – see below)*

Contents list

- List of numbered sections
- Page numbers

Executive summary

- What were the objectives?

- The findings of the research, in brief
- Conclusions from the findings
- Recommendations

Introduction

- Terms of reference

    (if not already presented)

- Need for & background to the report
- What procedure was followed
- What methods were used

    (e.g., experiments, interviews, etc)

- Acknowledgements
- Other sources

Body of report

- **The findings in detail**

Conclusions

- Assessment of evidence
- Deductions from findings
- Problems identified

Recommendations

- Suggested solutions to the identified problems

References

- Sources referred to in report

Bibliography

- Documents consulted but not referred to
- Further recommended reading

Appendices

- Less relevant but still useful matter
- Back-up material
- Copies of whatever research tools were used (e.g., questionnaires, letters, surveys, etc)
- Transcripts of interviews
- Other relevant reports in brief.

(An *informal* report, of course, may thankfully dispense with a lot of the above stuff, and an outline for such a simpler one is given on page 161.)

NB: This chapter necessarily duplicates much of the procedure for an in-depth feature, but is repeated here incorporating significant differences, and also so that the reader doesn't have to go back and forward between the two chapters.

Research

Your research varies according to the kind and depth of your report. Below are straightforward steps for an *in-depth* report: even though an informal report would require much less detail, these steps could still serve as a guide.

There are 10 phases to researching and writing a report:

A. Identify your readers

B. Determine the report's aims & objectives

C. Do background research

D. Gather information from sources

E. Assemble & winnow your material

F. Sort your material into categories

G. Put items in logical order

H. Develop written plan / outline

I. Write the report

J. Edit & check report

A. Identify your readers

Many a report fails utterly because its readers simply don't understand it. So the very first requirement, before any research or writing is undertaken, is to ascertain exactly who will read the report, and *what is the reader's level of expertise, experience, and technical knowledge.*

This is far from easy, as there may be several target readers with different such levels. It can be quite a balancing act to meet the needs of all of them. It may end in compromise, but those needs must be kept in mind, and met as far possible all through the following procedures.

B. Determine terms of reference

Clear terms of reference are essential before a report is undertaken. They are listed on page 141. Note that the *aim* of a report is a broad statement of the desired outcome. The *objective* is more than that – *it states exactly what will have been achieved when the report is finished* and should be included in the terms of reference. It must be crystal clear from the start.

It makes sense actually to state the objective in a single sentence, just to get clarity for writer and reader. Something like this: 'This report, when finished, will have identified the principal cause of the present situation, and will have outlined remedial steps to be taken.'

C. Do background research

1. **Open a file** containing whatever you have that is relevant. It should contain your preliminary notes and memos, cuttings from papers, photocopies of documents, query letters and replies, detailed results of surveys, experiments, and all relevant research.

It should include a rough draft of what you already know, and what you intend to do.

2. Do initial reading. Procedure here is identical to that for an in-depth feature. So purpose is (1) to ensure general broad grasp of subject (if you don't already have that); (2) to identify your informational and understanding gaps; (3) to identify where further reading is needed; (4) to know what preliminary questions to ask.

Sometimes a general book on the subject, or internet reports, can be a good starting point. But beware of getting lost in the reading, and failing to make the next step.

Also, research must be in proportion to importance and magnitude of the planned report. (And to its possible pay-off – in promotion or reputation).

3. *Prepare a list of preliminary questions* that need to be answered for you to write your report. They should at least deal with –

- The five Ws & H (what; where; who; when; why; and how). These are simply categories that help you cover the right questions.
- Persons relative to your report, and what information they can offer.
- Why the report is relevant *right now*.

D. Gather information from sources

1. List your sources. These vary widely according to what is being reported on, but are mostly as follows:

Personal sources

Colleagues

Informants

Personnel under study

Experts & consultants

Officialdom (gardai, civil servants, etc)

Yourself

(your own observation / experiments / questionnaires / interviews participant observation, etc)

Documentary sources

Internal files & memos

Records

Letters

Queries & responses

Questionnaires

Previous research / surveys / statistics

Publications: professional journals/ books

Abstracts

Electronic sources

Citation engines (See page 177)

Emails

Internet – Google/ Wikipedia/

Facebook/ Linkedin/ Twitter.

(all to be used with caution)

Restricted sites

CDs/ DVDs/ radio & TV documentaries

Electronic catalogues

Electronic records

NB. The degree to which you use your sources relates to the depth and gravity of your report. A simple record on Xmas spending might use only observation, whereas a report for a semi-state body or an academic journal would use much more. The following are typical sources:

Documents, **which can include –**

- Your own file contents;

- Further references from your reading;

- Existing reviews by consultants and others;

- Reviews commissioned from consultants;

- Minutes of meetings;

- Relevant government documents;

- Specialist periodicals that carry relevant reports. Libraries contain journals of abstracts, i.e., summaries of relevant reports, plus indications of where to find them. Librarians can direct you in this. We repeat here the warning that references can grow exponentially, as each one spawns perhaps 10 others – the *dendritic* phenomenon.

Experiments/ observations/ surveys/ interviews/ questionnaires

Reports involving the social sciences would most likely draw on surveys, observations; interviews;

questionnaires; participant observation. Pure science would stress experiments.

Citation engines

There are a number of extremely useful *citation engines* available on the internet. These are tools for finding information and referring to its source. They are explained on page 177. The most useful of all is *Google Scholar* – it's free; you don't have to log in; it's easy to use and it indexes a wide range of publications. There are lots of others, but many are specific to a particular discipline or science.

Persons

The key to successful report writing can often be the people who are approached and are willing to help. Such personal contacts include those with expertise, who can be established as consultants; those with personal experience of the situation who are willing to speak. (Can sometimes include whistle-blowers.) Establishing good will with such persons can often be crucial to a successful report. Sources can include –

• Personnel in institution being researched (from executives to workers on the ground);

- Outsiders who deal with such an institution;

- Professional organizations;

- Voluntary organizations;

- Interest groups; pressure groups; lobbies;

- Central- & local-government officials;

- Disgruntled citizens;

- Staff of trade magazines (Those in smaller magazines are often ready to talk);

•) Companies (especially their PR departments);

- Academia (The information offices of universities and institutes of technology can put you in touch with their resident expert);

- Librarians (often the best of all guides);

- Journalists who have covered the topic;

- Internet. There are websites dedicated to finding you the expert you need. They include *experts.com; expertisefinder.com; .profnet.com; newswise.com.* And Google can find you experts in particular disciplines. Simply type in *Experts in Sociology*, or whatever.

Note that one source can often provide several more. List them all, with phone numbers. Later you can decide which to use, selecting the most professional or most knowledgeable.

Organize your personal sources into categories. For example, in a report on a local road-safety issue, the categories could be – Gardai; local government officials; road engineers; outside consultants; medical personnel, and so on.

Prepare your list of questions, to be put to your sources. Different questions for different sources, and all aimed at eliciting the information or expertise your report needs.

Using your personal sources can involve telephoning, emailing or meeting. While telephoning or email can be sufficient, personal interviews invariably yield the best information, As with in-depth feature writing, the first contacts should be —

- those with the best knowledge;
- those most likely to be helpful;
- those who will be hardest to get (because it may take longer to get them).

Start at the top: begin with the best experts you can reach. Then work your way down.

When phoning a source, especially for the first time, have your questions written out beside you, so there is no hesitation. Keep questions brief, and to a minimum.

For face-to-face interviews, see page 119. And remember the final question: 'Is there anything else I should have asked you?'

Make sure you have the person's phone number and email, in case you need to check something later.

Take careful notes at the interview. Back these up with a small, unobtrusive recorder (preferably voice-activated).

E. Assemble & winnow the material

At a certain point, stop researching and assemble your material. At what point? *When the questions still unasked are mere details that can be checked later.* Proceed as with *In-depth features,* which procedure we repeat here for your convenience. Thus:

1. Winnow your material, cutting out what is not relevant. Take the relevant material from your

project file and place it in a new file marked *report file*.

2. Give an identifying number to each item and put it in square brackets [ ].

F. Sort into categories

Sort your material into categories, and give a brief name to each category, as shown below in italics. It helps if the categories are divided into three groups – (1) those essential to the argument; (2) non-essentials which can be used to back it up; and (3) peripheral items that may turn out to be useful.

In a report on road safety in a particular locality, some of the categories might be –

- Accident statistics over given period; *(stats)*
- Garda interviews, documents, etc *(garda)*
- Road layouts, and danger spots; *(layout)*
- Local residents' views; *(locals)*
- Notes from protest meeting; *(protests)*
- Local government views; *(govt)*
- Views of local road engineers; *(eng)*
- Outside consultants' views; *(consult)*
- Lack of road signs; *(signs)*

- Faulty or misleading road signs *(mislead)*
- Inappropriate speed limits; *(speed)*
- Financial limitations; *(finance)*
- Obstacles to improvements; *(obstacles)*
- Assessment of evidence; *(evidence)*
- Summary of problems; *(sum)*
- Proposed remedies; *(remedies)*

Now take each category, and prepare a list of the items that fit that category. Include the identifying number with each item.

G. Put items in logical order

Study the categories and their contents, until they form a pattern. An outline of the report will begin to grow in your mind, as you go back and forward through the categories.

The categories themselves often tell you how they relate and where they fit in the scheme of things.

H. Develop & write outline

As the outline grows, *write it down.* If, for example, it were a report on local road safety, the outline for the *Findings* section might look something like this, but certainly with considerably more detail –

> *Problem identified*
>> *High accident rate* [32, 48, 70]
>
> *Evidence from*
>> *Gardai* [17, 18, 23]
>>
>> *Residents* [36, 59, 33]
>>
>> *Records* [12]
>
> *Consultants' views* [112, 114, 120]
>
> *Probable factors*
>> *Problem layouts* [5, 22, 11]
>>
>> *Faulty signage* [3, 104, 88]
>>
>> *Official neglect* [43]
>
> *Financial constraints* [10, 97]

And so on. (Also take a look at pages 66 and 103 for further examples.)

The number beside each heading indicates the item in your file to which the heading refers.

I. Start writing

The report should be written to fit the formal structure shown on pages 141-142. *It is usually best to write the findings first;* then the conclusions and recommendations. The rest can be filled in after that. As each item in the outline is reached, use the identifying number (in square brackets) to fish out from your files whatever note, document, interview, or memo the number refers to. Write directly from that item.

A formal report differs from an in-depth feature article in one important respect – the manner of presentation. There are several standard formats for presenting a report's findings, the most popular being what is called the decimal system.

In this system each section is assigned a number (e.g., 2), and the subsections are numbered, 2.1, 2.2, 2.3 etc. Subsections of these are further numbered, e.g., 2.1.1, 2.1.2, 2.1.3.

As well as numbering, sections and subsections can be further identified by a hierarchy of type sizes and styles, as well as indentations. Something like this –

2. HEADING

2.1 First section

2.2 Second section

2.2.1 First subsection

2.2.2 Second subsection

And so on. The best way to understand this is to get hold of some finished report and model your format on it.

References

The methods or referencing in reports is normally specific to the institution requiring the report, and must be adhered to, as also in academic writing. Outside of such specific requirements, the simplest general way is to use the *Reference* facility of Word. It allows you to insert superscript numbers (like this – [2]), and then takes you to the end of the text, where the reference can be typed. The standard way of presenting references is – author's surname; first name or initial; title of book or paper (in italics); city & publisher; date; page number. Like this:

Soap, Joseph C. *How to Cheat in Exams.* London: Humbug & Co., 2018, pp. 132-135.

If the following reference is to the same source, simply write *Idem*, followed by the page numbers.

The above is just a fairly standard way to present references. However the different formats such as *Chicago/Turabian*, *APA* and *MLA* vary in their requirements. The simplest approach is often a citation engine called *Mendeley*. It will format the references for you exactly as required – *www.memdeley.com*. Or use *Endnote X8* – *www.endnote.com*. (See pages 177-179 for details on these citation engines. But don't break your heart over them unless you have to.)

Appendices can follow immediately on the main text, and can be used to present non-essential but useful information, samples of questionnaires or surveys which were used, and pointers for further research.

Executive summary

At the very end, write the *executive summary* (which you then place up at the start). In a couple of brief paragraphs it must grasp the absolute essentials of the report, nothing more, nothing less. It should be written in the knowledge *that it is probably the only bit that most people will ever read,* so it had better be spot on.

J. Edit & check the report

Next day, look at your report again (at least 24 hours later, if possible). Take off your writer's hat, and put on your editor's hat. Check all the items listed on pages 141-142.

It is advisable to edit three times. First for *content* – completeness, accuracy, attribution and references. Second time for the *mechanics* – spelling and punctuation – and the third time for *format* – paragraphing, headings, pagination, professional appearance, and so on.

Get at least two colleagues or peers to review the report and give you feedback. Preferably several.

There are various formats for the finished document, and you must select the one that is customary in the institution for which you are writing. A fairly standard one would be on A.4 pages, printed in 12pt Times New Roman (<- like this), with 1.5-line spacing. Headings can range from 24pt down to 12pt, varying from italic to bold or both, as required.

The document can be comb bound, wire bound, ring bound, slide bound, or professionally printed and bound in book format, if it's terribly important (like some of those CYA cover-your-ass government reports that nobody ever reads).

Informal reports

If it sounds like writing, I rewrite it
—Elmore Leonard

INFORMAL reports vary in structure, but can be considered as slimmed-down versions of formal reports. Here is a simple outline for an informal report:

On title page or top of first page

- The word *Memorandum*
- Brief descriptive title
- Author's name
- Confidentiality note (if required)
- Date

Introduction & terms of reference

- Report requested by...
- Written by...
- For what readership?
- Aims and objective of the report
- Procedures followed

Body of the report

- *Findings*

Conclusions

- Deductions from findings
- Key facts
- Identification of problems

Recommendations

- Suggested solutions to the problems which have been identified

Author's name and signature.

Writing a school essay

Anyone who is going to be a writer knows
enough at 15 to write several novels
—May Sarton

THERE are various kinds of school essay, including telling a story of some incident that happened to you, or describing a film or play – but the most frequent is making a case for something, such as – *Mobile phones do more harm than good*; or *Transition year is a waste of time*. It's often called an opinion piece.

The earlier chapters on effective writing skills, on feature writing and the 19 intros, are all relevant for a school essay. Note especially what was said about brevity – short sentences and paragraphs. Take a look at those chapters one more time before reading further here.

Opinion essays
There is a simple technique for this type of essay.

First: on a notepad write the topic and your opinion in a single sentence for or against – agreeing or disagreeing with the topic. E.g., *mobile phones are our best friend (after our doggie)*.

Put this at the top of the page. Below that write everything you can think of to back up your statement about mobile phones, using just a phrase or a couple of words for each point. E.g. –

- *Keeps folks in touch;*
- *Cure for loneliness;*
- *Great for games;*
- *Siri answers my queries;*
- *Can learn from Google;*
- *Camera always ready;*
- *Can make videos;*
- *Tunes galore;*
- *Fabulous flash lamp;*
- *Help in emergency;*
- *Can record crimes; etc*

Then, on a separate sheet of paper, pick out your *three best points*, and develop each. Express each one fully, and then back it up with one or two examples to prove your point. (If you are handwriting the essay and are unsure of your intro at the start, a good idea is to leave a space at the top to insert your intro later.)

These examples can take the form of a mini-narrative (similar to the intro on page 22). E.g. —

> An example of the usefulness of mobile phones was when two Alabama policemen proceeded to beat a black man to death last year. They were filmed by a student using his mobile phone. It led to their prosecution and conviction.

Then move on to the next point, in a new paragraph. Connect the paragraphs with words or phrases like *furthermore…, another reason for this is…* , and so on.

You can develop this second point with another example, or with a quotation from a poem or from some authority. And the same with your third point.

Then write a final paragraph, once more making your point that mobile phones are a person's best friend. End with a good strong sentence, or a quotation, or one more example to prove your point. Or even something humorous, if it seems to fit.

Now go back to the top and put an opening sentence or paragraph, if not already done, using one of the 19 intros listed on page 22 and following pages.

And, as always, indent each paragraph, except the first one. And put the very first word in capital letters. Do this even if the essay is handwritten. However if you have access to a laptop, use it.

Prescribed texts

Essays on novels, poems or Shakespeare plays can also be considered opinion pieces – your opinion on what the author intended, or how effective the author was, or what most moved you on reading the story or seeing the play. So they too can follow the above guidelines for opinion pieces.

The main difference is that they require quotations from the text to back up the opinion, so it is always recommended to have some quotes off by heart, especially coming up to exams.

However the most important point is to understand exactly what is being asked, and respond to it as precisely and carefully as possible.

Essays in an exam

In an exam situation, you will have far less time to prepare your thoughts. Nevertheless, the above technique can work here too. Get your ideas down as already shown on one sheet, as fast as you can. Then number them in the order you want to use them.

Cross out that page with a large X, so that the examiner realises it's not for assessment. Then start your essay on the next sheet, and proceed as shown above.

(Regarding the preliminary notes that you crossed out – sometimes even these will impress the examiner, indicating that you actually planned your essay.)

How they mark you

Papers are marked using four criteria (known as *PCLM*):

Purpose (focus; relevance; specific structure; staying on the task);

Coherence (how well the paragraphs and sentences follow from each other, and whether the essay has a logical sense of progression overall);

Language effectiveness (using the appropriate language and register for the specific task at hand – a good racy style describing a competitive sports event; a calmer gentler style depicting a sunset or a painting. And remember *fluency, clarity, brevity*;

Mechanics (punctuation, spelling & grammar).

Technical essays

Answers to questions in other exam subjects, such as science or sociology, can be dealt with in a similar way – getting the ideas down fast, and then putting them in order before starting to write.

However there is one difference – most of the 19 intros (narrative, shock, etc) have little place in technical writing. The only one that really works is the *summary intro* in which you briefly outline the points you intend to make, and then develop each one. (See page 28.)

Narrative essays

Essays like *My most memorable experience*, or *Our Vacation in the Algarve*, are best written by isolating the high moments, rather than just telling one durn thing after another. Ignore the boring bits.

It is in such essays that the above chapters on observation and sense of wonder particularly come into play (pages 109 and 115).

Call on all your senses – the intense blue of that sky; the strains of gipsy music heard from the balcony; smells wafting from restaurants; lashing winds and crashing seas.

But above all, what you saw is far less important than *how you felt when you saw it.* Your sense of wonder at *The Mona Lisa*; your awe at the Grand Canyon; your terror when that plane hit such turbulence.

As always, keep your best bit for the intro. Often a narrative or descriptive intro will fit nicely – the sheer joy you experienced when you felt that tug on the line during that fishing trip. Or a quote from Joseph Plunkett – *His body gleams amid eternal snows* – if you have been off on a skiing holiday.

And, by the way, take a look at the following pages on academic essays – there's some stuff there that might also be helpful.

Note: Some schools send out their students to interview interesting local people. The students encounter utterly novel ideas, meet people they might never have spoken to, and it results in some really marvellous writing. (See page 119 about how to interview.)

Epigraphs

Have you noticed the little quote at the start of each chapter in this book? It's called an *epigraph,* and is simply a quote from someone well known, which serves to hint at what is to come. And to lighten things a bit.

An epigraph can be impressive at the head of your essay. It suggests how widely read you are (even if you're not). Or at least that you took the trouble to look for a worthwhile quote.

But where can you find such quotes, especially if you're not that well read? Well, here's a little secret, but don't tell teacher. Let's say you are writing an essay on 'Teenage angst'. Simply go to Google and type in *Quotes on teenage angst.* I've just done that, and here are some of what I found—

Now when I was a teenager, I was angsty as any teenager was, but after 17 years of having a mother who was in and out of my life like a yo-yo and a father who was faceless, I was angry

— Jarrett J. Krosoczka

'Now, Sophia, would you care to tell me why you're here by the pond instead of reporting to your next class?' 'I'm experiencing some teenage angst, Mrs. Casnoff,' I answered. 'I need to, like, write in my journal or something'

—Rachel Hawkins

Teenage... the time in life when you show your individuality by looking like everyone else

—Simi Ngr

I don't know what better teenage life you could get than going around the world doing what you love to do

—Anna Kournikova

Let's face it. No kid in high school feels as though they fit in

—Stephen King

I was a quiet teenager, introverted, full of angst

—Nigella Lawson

Teenage boys, goaded by their surging hormones,
run in packs like the primal horde. They have only
a brief season of exhilarating liberty between
control by their mothers and control by their wives

—Camille Paglia

Led Zeppelin has been there through three
generations of teenage angst. And there's a
generation of kids now who won't know it, post-
Linkin Park

—Author: Robert Plant

Americans invented adolescence. It is not a natural
phenomenon. Adolescence is a social construct,
created by an urban-industrial society that keeps
its young at home far past puberty. Teenage angst
is a luxury if a successful modern human conceit
that isn't condoned by our superior species

— Sarah Beth Durst

I think every teenager goes through their angst.
People who are like, 'No, I had a perfect
adolescence,' make me wonder how that is possible

—Shailene Woodley

Under 18 there are no ugly girls

—Chinese proverb

Now just imagine one of those quotes at the head of your essay...

Sometimes too your quotes are right in front of you, in the lyric of your favourite song or even the quotes you've already learnt in English class. That quote from *Hamlet* or *Wuthering Heights* could be the perfect start to your essay.

Academic writing

*I am returning this otherwise good typing paper to you
because someone has printed gibberish all over it
and put your name at the top*
—Professor of English,
Ohio University

ACADEMIC writing differs in one essential from most other non-fiction: it is aimed at a 'discourse community' – that is, a group of people who have common interests and disciplines. Examples – academic faculty, researchers, scientists, students, members of the professions such as law, medicine, engineering, social science, psychology, philosophy, electronics, marine biology, and so on.

These groups all have constraints and conventions on how writing is to be presented. The problem however is they differ from one another in exactly what style, convention and formality they require. So, if you are writing within one of these disciplines, the first thing is to become familiar with its required style.

There are a number of standard styles used by these communities, mostly created in the US. Principally they are the *APA* (American Psychological Association), the *MLA* (Modern Language Association), the *Harvard Style*, and the *Chicago Manual of Style* (Kate L. Turabian). Each has its strict rules for paragraphing, footnoting, citing sources, in-text citations, references to books and to the Internet. You need to ascertain which discipline uses which style. You can then find that style, and even a template, in Google. Just type 'APA' or whatever. We also recommend a careful study of previous articles or dissertations within your discipline.

We obviously cannot cover all these styles here, but what we can best do is to give general pointers on what is common to most academic writing. So here goes.

Function

The function of academic writing is (1) to introduce a new concept, or (2) to explore or reinforce an existing concept, or (3) to challenge that concept. It is an impersonal communication to an informed discourse community, referring to previous research, but taking it further. It takes certain 'facts' for granted (facts in this case being things the community takes as given, and that do not therefore require proof). Such writing is expected to be more formal and impersonal than a magazine feature. And, while the research methods can be similar to those for an in-depth feature or a report, the construction of such writing follows certain standard requirements.

Citation engines

The Internet has a number of extremely useful tools, called *citation engines.* These are essentially tools for digging out information and referring it to its source.

A useful one is *Google Scholar* – it's free; it's easy to use, and it indexes a wide range of publications.

According to its website, Google Scholar provides a simple way broadly to search for scholarly literature. From one place, you can search across many disciplines and sources: articles, theses, books, abstracts and court opinions, from academic publishers, professional societies, online repositories, universities and other web sites. Google Scholar helps you find relevant work across the world of scholarly research.

Under the heading *Search*, Google Scholar provides guidelines to help you find recent papers, locate the full text of an article, and get effective answers to your queries.

There is also *Mendeley*, a desktop and web program for managing and sharing research papers, accessing research data and collaborating online. It allows you to import articles with one click, to organise them and choose in which of your files to save them. With the Mendeley *Reference Manager*, you can easily organize and search your personal library and annotate documents. You can cite as you write, using Mendeley's *Citation Plugin*.

There are lots of others citation engines, but many are specific to a particular discipline or science. Here are a few –

- *arXiv* (sciences)
- *rePEc* (economics)
- *CiteseerX* (computer and IT)

- *Publish or Perish* (information management)

When it comes to referencing, *Citation Machine*™ is an effective tool, which finds your source, and then enables you to properly credit the information that you use. As the website says, 'Its primary goal is to make it so easy for researchers to cite their information sources, that there is virtually no reason not to.'

One of the most useful tools of all must surely be *Endnote X8* (www.endnote.com). It doesn't quite write your stuff for you, but it's certainly handy. A product of Thomson Reuters, it enables you to search, create, find and share resources; to organize references as you download them; to create groups via drag & drop; to share groups; to import PDFs; to find full texts of articles; to attach related files; to cite references as you write, via a built-in tool, and automatically create a bibliography.

The simpler *Endnote Basic* can be downloaded free. However *Endnote X8* costs money – full cost is nearly €300, but there are reductions for students and groups. You can download a free trial on the website, and there is also a short film to explain how it all works. For queries on Endnote, researchers in Ireland should contact *Bilaney Consultants* in Sevenoaks, Kent – telephone 00.44.1732.450.002.

Acceptable & not

A lot of the things frowned upon in these pages – use of the passive voice; long paragraphs; dependent clauses; words from the Latin – are unfortunately acceptable here. Indeed, expected. There is also, as stated earlier, a standardised system of referencing within each discipline.

Of course each discipline uses terminology that no layperson might understand, but this is acceptable since such words are common currency for readers in that discourse community. (That of course should not excuse medics like Doc Martin using those big words to his terrified patients.)

Also, a lot of things we recommended earlier are unacceptable here – humour, use of *you* or *I*, *don't, won't and isn't*. Except that the use of the vertical pronoun *(I)* is considered acceptable in social-science research. But forget those 19 intros, except perhaps the summary one.

The problem is that all this formality can unfortunately be taken to extremes, resulting in downright obscurity. There is an anonymous 16th century quote that says, *He that useth many words for explaining any subject doth, like the cuttlefish, hide himself in his own ink.*

Publisher and Voice of America editor Sol Stein puts it in a more modern context: *Much academic writing is counter-educational because its dullness insulates its information from nearly everybody.*

Academic writing roughly falls into two categories – (1) college-level essays, dissertations and projects; and (2) the writing for professional or 'learned' journals.

College essays

College essays frequently follow a structure developed in the USA, and fall into three parts – the introduction, the body of the essay, and the conclusion.

Introduction: The first paragraph starts with a general statement on the topic, perhaps with a quote, fact or paraphrase from some authority, and moves directly to the main thesis of the essay. Essentially it says what the essay is about, and sets a limit to the topic. The final sentence should if possible hook into the following paragraph.

Body: The following three to four paragraphs carry the main arguments, one per paragraph. Preferably in descending order of importance.

Each paragraph is best developed by an example, a quote from authority, statistical evidence, or a point of logic. It should end if possible with a link or 'hook' to the next paragraph.

Any reference to authority is normally followed by the author's surname and date in brackets – e.g., *(Trumpington, 1987)*.

Conclusion: This final paragraph winds up the argument, summarises the main points, restates the thesis (in slightly different words from the original statement in the introduction), and may add some final thoughts. In certain cases (such as an ethical topic) there might be a place here for suggestions for actions to be taken.

Note: If you have referred to research, or have quoted some authority, credit must be given after the conclusion, by placing a list of these references at the end of the text. You can use the simple method shown on page 158, putting footnotes into the text and completing them at the end. (Microsoft Word will enable footnotes if you click on *References*.) But remember that the certain disciplines demand different approaches to referencing. So the use of a citation engine may be the answer. (See page 177.)

This college-essay format, however, is not cherished everywhere, and is sometimes derided as 'the hamburger format' – the intro being the top bun, followed by the meat, the sauce, the dill pickles and the slice of cheese, rounded off with the bottom bun (the conclusion). However we believe it can be of help to students who are starting in academia. Worth trying, anyhow.

Constructing a paragraph

If a paragraph contains several sentences, they can be set out as shown below (hamburger format again):

Topic sentence. This first sentence states what the paragraph is about. It should be simple, brief, and contain just the one idea – the most important idea (the 'bottom line' at the top). Ideally it should also reverse-link to the previous paragraph, using a phrase like *This is because...*

Supporting sentences. These develop the topic of the first sentence; may argue the point; add further information or evidence; and give further ideas that flow from the topic.

Concluding sentence winds up the argument and sums it up. If possible it should hook itself to the following paragraph, using a phrase like *This however is more dangerous than had hitherto been suspected*. The reader naturally moves on to ask why.

In essence, a paragraph is a miniature of the whole essay format. This paragraph structure can be useful, not just for academic essays, but for features and most other forms of writing.

Plagiarism

There, we've mentioned the P word. Nearly didn't. Plagiarism is perhaps the greatest source of ruin for so many budding academic writers.

Also referred to as 'heavy lifting', plagiarism is defined by the Oxford Dictionary as 'the practice of taking someone else's work or ideas, and passing them off as one's own'.

The best advice is *just don't*. It seems so easy, especially with all this lovely stuff on the Internet. But just remember that the authorities also have the Internet, and all sorts of lovely stuff with which to catch you out.

And yet plagiarism is so often perpetrated in all innocence. The key therefore is *passing something off as one's own*. All of us take the ideas of others – but we take them to build upon them, discuss them, develop them. Otherwise there would be little progress in any discipline.

The solution is *always to acknowledge*. Simplest way is to put the author's name and date in brackets *(Trumpington, 1987)*, and then put the full reference in the footnotes.

It's not always that simple, of course. If one has been studying or teaching or working with something over many years, many concepts can be absorbed and become taken for granted – as one's own. Really the only way to deal with this problem is to acknowledge that possibility in an introduction, and ask pardon of all and sundry. (I have done exactly that on page 7 – necessary after a total of 38 years teaching journalism and writing skills.)

And, by the way, in academic writing, ignore what we said on page 41 about unacknowledged quotes. *Just acknowledge everything, period.*

'The learned journals'

A great deal of new thinking and scientific development comes via those periodicals that cater to the various professions and academic disciplines – popularly known as 'the learned journals'. Their function is to present the findings of research, enquiries and fieldwork; to outline new theories or discoveries; to present new models of policy or practice; or to offer new insights or perspectives into already accepted ideas – referred to as 'entering the conversation' or 'adding to the debate'.

An article in one of these journals usually presents such findings in the form of a clear argument backed by evidence, but that also draws on a range of references and previous reports and research, to substantiate what is presented, and to outline the pros and cons. It is this wider referencing that essentially differs it from a straightforward report. It does however resemble a report in that it has an executive summary – in this case referred to as the *Abstract*.

Requirements

Each of these journals has its own stringent requirements in style and presentation, which must be carefully studied and followed.

These requirements can be found on the journal's website, and are often referred to as 'the house style'.

Such journals invariably require that any article written for them be evaluated and passed by other professionals before publication. This is known as 'peer review'.

Academese

One of the hazards of academic writing is falling into the trap of *academese* – in other words, writing gobbledy-gook instead of genuine English. It's usually when someone is using big words while trying to be 'formal'. Lionel Trilling calls it *non-thought*:

> A spectre haunts our culture – it is that people will eventually be unable to say, 'They fell in love and married,' let alone understand the language of *Romeo and Juliet*, but will as a matter of course say 'Their libidinal impulses being reciprocal, they activated their individual erotic drives

and integrated them within the same frame
of reference.'

In times past the lives of sociology students, including myself, were made miserable by having to read the almost unreadable meanderings of sociologist Talcott Parsons. He has some fine ideas, presumably, but to extract those ideas from his prose was like digging for jewels in an underground mine. We all thought his thinking must be so brilliant that it must be almost beyond our comprehension. Now I realise the fellow simply couldn't write.

Whether we like it or not, being an expert in some area of learning does not necessarily mean being able to write English. Academia and the learned journals are littered with utterly unreadable stuff, often by folks who think they are being 'formal'. Dan Simmons describes a colleague as 'crippled by the need to write in academese. It is not a language formed by any human tongue, and few, if any, academics survive the degradation of it to move on to actual prose.'

We also get such horrors in the written or verbal utterances of government officials. However sometimes, alas, these are content to continue in their unreadable and unspeakable ways, as a little bit of obscurity can at times be extremely helpful. To them, of course. Not to us.

And we'll say nothing about lawyers, or about insurance companies when they write that small print, with its legalese and cover-your-ass clauses. Or gabble that fast talk at the end of radio adverts. CYA again – 'we don't give a damn whether you understood it or not. Point is, we *said* it.'

Last word: *Is it possible to decrivate the concanics of unimodal socification, through a process of consortitive sectification, as far as the ultivacular fractiles can corrive?*

Well, is it?

Or isn't it?[*]

---

[*] See page 217

Writing a speech

Fear of public speaking can be overcome with effective
speaking tips, skills and strategies
—Robert Moment

ONE of the nice things about writing for publication is that you're usually not around when someone reads it. Unfortunately speech writing is different – you have to face those rows and rows of impassive faces staring up at you as you deliver. And that's what daunts so many of us.

Yet a carefully written speech and effective notes can make the ordeal so much easier – it eliminates hesitation, and gives confidence.

Four ways

There are four basic ways to approach a speech:

- Write the whole speech and learn it by heart;
- Write the whole speech and read it;

- Write the whole speech, but speak
  from notes;
- Don't write the speech, but just speak
  from notes.

Which approach is better? It all depends on one's experience, fluency, spontaneity, level of confidence. And, of course, the kind of audience you have. Let's look at each approach.

• *Learn the speech by heart.* Generally not recommended, even though it is practised in so many debating societies. The effort to remember every single word so concentrates the mind that the speaker misses out on spontaneity, on relating to the audience, and on a sense of ease.

• *Read the speech.* Can be effective, provided that the speaker regularly looks up at the audience. If not, there can be a failure to relate to the listeners.

None of us were present at Gettysburg, but one can guess that Lincoln's exquisitely crafted three-minute speech was written and rewritten, pared to perfection before delivery. But we can also guess that at regular intervals he fixed that famous gaze upon his audience, as when he said:

The world will little note nor long remember what we say here, but it can never forget what they did here...

He was wrong there – the world *did* note and remembers to this day those incomparable words.

• **Write but use notes**. For most of us, this gives more spontaneity, and helps us relate to our audience. Especially if we look at the notes and back to the audience all the time.

I suggest that, if you use this approach, you use very simple headings, which serve to remind you of what to say next.

There as two ways to do this – (1) use a pile of stiff note-cards, with a heading on each, which you work your way through and put aside as you go along. Or (2) use a single sheet (preferably an A.4 folded longways), with the headings one below the other, written large, even in capitals, just a couple of words each, so that the speaker need only glance down to see what comes next.

If it were the Gettysburg speech, the headings might be –

NEW NATION

NOW CIVIL WAR

MET ON BATTLEFIELD

DEDICATE

WE CANNOT...

And so on. We have no idea if Lincoln did this, but he may well have done.

If you use this approach, I suggest that, after writing the speech, you practice with the text in front of you, but using your notes as far as possible. After a while you should find the notes are almost enough.

However when actually delivering the speech from notes, it is still wise to keep the full text on the lectern so that, if you forget or hesitate, it's all right there. This is particularly important for novice speakers as it gives assurance.

• *Just speak from notes.* It may seem daunting, but many speakers, as they grow in confidence, prefer this approach. It allows more spontaneity, which matters so much in public speaking. It also allows flexibility, allowing the speaker to deal more easily with questions and heckling.

Suggestion: Use television to watch the various speakers in the Dail or Westminster, to see which approach they use. We can learn so much from the pros.

Opening a speech

The essential difference between a speech and a published article is that a speaker has a captive audience. Whereas a reader can drift off to something else after the first few words, your listeners will stay for at least a while (even if they do finally get up and walk out).

This means there are two ways of opening a speech.

1. The 19 intros. The first is to use one of *the 19 standard intros* (pages 22-34) to grab the listeners, just as you would in a written piece. In fact it's usually the most effective way to start.

In the ferocious winter of 1954, the late Abbé Pierre began his talk on Radio Luxembourg with the words –

> A woman froze to death tonight at 3 a.m., on the pavement of Sebastopol Boulevard, clutching the eviction notice which the day before had made her homeless... Each night, more than two thousand endure the cold,

without food, without bread, more than one almost naked. To face this horror, emergency lodgings are not enough...

The media in the following days wrote of an 'uprising of kindness' *(insurrection de la bonté)* and resulted in the raising of 500 million francs for relief. Charlie Chaplin gave two million.

The *Question intro* is one of the most effective for a speech. Asking what is to be done about something that everyone is concerned about, can be a marvellous opening. Provided of course you have an answer, and that you reach it fairly quickly.

2. Slow burn. The second way to open a speech is called the *slow burn*. Because of your captive audience, you can start quietly with something quite commonplace, and gradually work up to what you want to get across.

Hitler was a genius at this. He would begin with something slow and quiet about how noble were the decent upstanding Volk of Germany, and gradually work up to a final screaming rant about the Versailles Treaty and those dastardly French, and what the Nazis were going to do about them – ending with –

> I, the Führer, if I have to lie, I will lie for the good of the Greater German People! If I have to betray, I will betray for the good of the Greater German People! If I have to kill, I will kill for the good of the Greater German People! *Ein Volk, ein Reich, ein Führer...*

By which time the audience are all on their feet bellowing *Sieg Heil! Sieg Heil! SIEG HEIL!* Note, by the way, the power of repetition in the above speech, which would be out of place in a printed piece.

Unless however you plan to be a dictator, you mightn't want to orate precisely like the Führer. But the slow burn can certainly work, provided it's not too long drawn out. A good example is the *Surprise intro* on page 31, where the audience is told that young people nowadays have no sense of duty, etc. etc., until we learn that this is a quote from Peter the Hermit from the year 1095.

Kinds of speech

A speech can have many different functions, and obviously the approach is different for each. It can be ceremonial, including a funeral oration or the Best Man's speech at a wedding. It can be a protest speech outside the Dail. Or a political speech inside the Dail. Or a speech asking for donations. Or a lecture to educate or inform.

A few suggestions

Keep *all* speeches as brief as possible. As Stephen Keague says, 'No audience ever complained about a presentation or speech being too short.'

• *Speaking at a funeral,* keep in mind that you are addressing people who are grieving. Give a very brief life history of the deceased, stressing achievements and interests – academic, business, literary, sporting – family relationships, your memories. If the deceased was not particularly nice, pick out some *believable* good points – there are always some – but don't exaggerate or you'll irritate. Offer sympathy to the close relatives *by name.* And keep it short. (When preparing the speech it can help to contact family members who can suggest topics to mention.)

The most difficult and delicate speech of all is at the funeral of one who has taken his or her own life. Indeed, in giving a few pointers here, I could be in danger of trivialising the tragedy. But a few points do need to be made.

Firstly, say something to ease the sense of guilt and failure of the close relatives. Secondly, do not *ever* show the deed as heroic, or praise the deceased too much. Especially in the death of a younger person, such praise can provoke others to imitate. Thirdly, if the family belongs to any religious group, go unhesitatingly to that group's scripture (Bible, Torah or Quran), where there are always sacred words that bring much consolation. Fourthly – unless there is a danger of offending a non-believing family – do make a reference to the infinite mercy of God, as the key thing to be remembered in such a tragedy.

If you need help in preparing a speech in these circumstances, there is considerable guidance in Google. Just type in – *Funeral message for suicide.)*

• *As Best Man* at a wedding, your main function is ceremonial. In other words, it has to be gone through, like it or lump it. It is most easily got through by gently entertaining the listeners. So try if you can to be humorous without being vulgar. And never, *ever,* tell tales about the groom's escapades in the past.

Start by saying who you are, and how well you know and respect the groom (even if you don't). But remember, it's about them, not you. Say something nice about the bride, admitting that perhaps you don't know her that well, if that's the case, but that you hope to. Congratulate the groom but not the bride, to whom you simply wish years of happiness (the convention being that the groom is fortunate to have won the lady, but that the lady could have had any fellow she chose). And then go straight to the toast. To a wonderful couple and all that. And keep it short. *Please.* Two minutes is best.

• *When lecturing to inform or teach*, do <u>not</u> use Powerpoint unless it is absolutely necessary to illustrate something that cannot otherwise be made clear. Using a screen with bullet points, simply to show the points you are about to make, just irritates listeners. There's such a thing as 'death by Powerpoint'.

• *In speaking to persuade*, try to match your language to your listeners. Remember Lee Iacocca's words:

Talk to people in their own language. If you do it well, they'll say, 'God, he said exactly what I was thinking.' And when they begin to respect you, they'll follow you to the death.

And again try something you daren't do in print – repeat the main point over and over, to hammer it in. Remember Hitler? Or, as Churchill put it –

If you have an important point to make, don't try to be subtle or clever. Use a pile driver. Hit the point once. Then come back and hit it again. Then hit it a third time – a tremendous whack !

Rick Sherrell puts it even more succinctly –

Tell 'em what you're gonna tell 'em –
Then tell 'em –
Then tell 'em what you told 'em.

And, once again, learn from the pros. Listen to their speeches on TV. The ones who can *really* communicate. Not the others.

Ending a speech

The function of the final words of a speech depends on the aim of the speech – to persuade, convince, console, inform, entertain, rouse, edify, or whatever. The 19 intros once again can be called into play, just as they were for a printed piece.

But their main function once again is to put hooks into the listeners, so that they carry away with them the thoughts that you presented.

Grammar is dead easy

I never made a mistake in grammar but one in my life
and as soon as I done it I seen it
—Carl Sandburg

MANY of us are unsure of our grammar when we write. Yet we use it perfectly well when we speak. So it's only a question of knowing what kinds of words we are using, and why we use them in a particular way. If it's explained simply, it can be understood in half a day. The following is really all we need to know.

Parts of speech

Very, very simply, they're all about *things* and *what they do*. Such as a dog biting a child –

> The shaggy dog runs quickly
> and it bites a child.

There is the thing itself – ***dog*** – which needs to be singled out from other dogs and made definite –

the dog. So what kind of dog is it? It's **shaggy**. And what does the dog do? It **runs**. Just how does it run? It runs **quickly.** Anything else? Yes: **And it bites a child.** So here's the sentence that says all that—

The (*definite article* singles out this *definite* dog, not just any old dog)

shaggy (*adjective* describes the dog)

dog (*noun* is the main player, the *subject* that does it all)

runs (*verb* says what the dog does)

quickly (*adverb* says just *how* the dog runs)

and (*conjunction* joins to next bit, telling you there's more damage to come)

it (*pronoun* stands in for the noun *dog*)

bites (another *verb*, this time with an unfortunate victim or *object*)

a (*indefinite article* says we're *not definite* as to which wretched child)

child. (another *noun,* which is the *object* of the biting).

These are simply the words we use, like nouns, verbs, adjectives, adverbs, and so on. So what could be simpler? All we need to do is consider each of these different sorts of words, plus one or two more. Here they are—

NOUN – the name of a thing or a person.
It can be –

- ***Proper*** – name of a *particular* thing or person *(Market Street; Maggie; Carlow)*, written <u>with</u> a capital; or
- ***Common*** – name of something *in general (street; woman; county)*, written <u>without</u> a capital.

Common nouns can be –

- ***Abstract*** – non-tangible things – qualities *(honesty)*; emotions *(joy)*; state or condition *(old age)*; or
- ***Concrete*** – things you can touch, see, hear, smell or feel *(rock; planet; noise; wind; doggie)*.

PRONOUN – a word that takes the place of a noun *(it; she; who)*. It can be –

- *Personal* (I; me; you; he; she; him; her). This can be –
    - ➢ **Subjective**, or the doer (I; he; she); or
    - ➢ **Objective**, or the one done to (me; him; her).
- **Interrogative** – asking a question, interrogating (who? what?);
- *Reflexive* – referring back to the doer (he hurt <u>himself</u>);
- *Relative* – relating to someone or something that went before (who; which; that);
- *Indefinite* – referring to nothing in particular (anyone; none).

VERB – states what the noun *is* or *does*. Here's what a verb can do—

- It can have a doer (John walks) – and is called a *finite verb*; or
- It can have *no* doer (<u>to</u> walk) – and is called *non-finite*. There are three such –
    - ➢ to walk *(infinitive)*;
    - ➢ walking *(present participle)*;
    - ➢ walked *(past participle)*.

A verb can do the following –

- It can make a statement or *indicate* something *(I hate you; there it is)*, and is called **indicative**; or

- Give an order *(Get lost)*, and is called **imperative**; or

- Ask a question, or *interrogate* someone *(What are you up to?)*, so is called **interrogative**; or

- Express a *condition (If you do that...)* and is called **conditional**; or

- Express something hypothetical, unlikely, hoped for *(If I were you; Come what may...; So be it; God save the Queen; I wish you were dead)* and is called **subjunctive.**

These five kinds of expression are called **moods.**

If a verb has an object (e.g., *bites* a child), it's called **transitive.** If no object, (e.g., *runs*), it's called **intransitive.**

As life has a past, present and future, so has every verb – it's called its **tense** –

- *I go* **(present tense)**
- *I went* **(past tense)**;

- *I shall go (**future tense**)* (nowadays in Ireland mostly mutating to *I <u>will</u> go* – although strictly speaking that means '*I'm determined to go.* But nobody seems to bother with the distinction any more).

These tenses can be **simple** *(I go)*; **continuing** *(I am going)*; **completed** *(I have gone)*.

A verb can also be –

- **active** *(Mary hit Ger),* where Mary acts; or
- **passive** *(Ger was hit by Mary),* where poor Ger just suffers passively.

These are called the verb's **voice** (active & passive voices). The passive voice is beloved of officialdom, as a way of avoiding responsibility. (*It was deemed advisable* – who did the deeming?)

ARTICLE – There are only three *(the, a, an)* –

- The word *the* picks out something and makes it *definite (<u>the</u> big man)*, so it's called the **definite article.**
- The word *a* or *an* leaves it vague *or indefinite (<u>a</u> big man; <u>an</u> orange)*, so it's called the **indefinite article.**

ADJECTIVE – describes a noun *(a fast car)*.

It can –

   —do just that – describe – *(a fast car)* and is called **positive**; or

   —compare it with others *(a faster car)* so is called **comparative**; or

   —make it the very top *(the fastest car)*, so is called **superlative.**

These are called *adjectives of degree*.

There are some other adjectives that point things out (*that* man; *this* car), and are called **demonstrative**.

Some show ownership or possession (*my* man; *his* car) and are called **possessive.**

ADVERB – it simply adds more to the meaning of an adjective (an <u>unusually</u> big man); or to the meaning of a verb (he runs *quickly*); or of another adverb (he runs <u>very</u> quickly).

PREPOSITION – words like *of, with, by, for, to,* have the job of joining words to get meaning *(book <u>of</u> fiction; come <u>with</u> me; that's <u>for</u> me; come <u>to</u> me).* It can join phrases as well as words *(she is the best looking <u>of</u> all who are here).*

CONJUNCTION – *(and, but, or, if, as)* creates a join or *junction* of two words or groups of words *(you or me; Joe and I; I'll go if you stay; It's as I promised; You love him but I hate the creep)*. And it's OK nowadays to start a sentence with *and* or *but*. We just did.

And that's all we really need to know about parts of speech.

Who, which, that

Many people fear these relative pronouns, but five very simple basic rules can make sense of them:

1) Use **who** or **whom** in all instances when it refers to *a person*. E.g. –

The girl *who runs the show* is in hospital.

The girl *whom I kissed* is in hospital.

Note that *who* refers to the person acting (*runs the show*), whereas *whom* refers to the person suffering an action (*being kissed*), or being acted upon.

2) Use **that** for a thing, a non-person (i.e., a dog, place, phone, etc), *when it is used to identify the thing.* E.g. –

The phone *that you stole* is on the table.
I.e., no other phone but the stolen one.

But if it is a person, use **who** or **whom**. E.g.,

The red-haired girl, *whom kissed*, is in hospital.

3) Use **which** when it does not identify the thing, *but is an additional thought.* E.g. –

The red phone which, by the way, you stole, is on the table.

Here I am not identifying the phone by the fact that you stole it. I identify it by its red colour. I then simply add the *extra* fact that you stole it.

Even if I omit the words 'by the way', this still holds true. E.g. –

The red phone, which you stole, is on the table.

This fact, which you omit, condemns you.

4) Use **which** when it follows a preposition (*to, for, with,* etc) –

The town *to which* I am going...

The cause *for which* he died...

The gun *with which* I killed him...

You couldn't say 'the gun with that I killed him'. However you *could* say 'the gun that I killed him with' –   if you don't mind ending with a preposition. (Better simply stop the killing. – Ed)

5) However, following rule 1 above, if it's a person, you would use **whom** --

The girl *to whom* I gave it...

The girl *with whom* I went home...

Building a sentence

Take your hands off my sentences, asshole.
I sweat blood for that shit
— Scott Adlerberg

A SENTENCE is a group of words (or even a single word) *that actually says something* – a statement; a question; a command; an agreement). It begins with a capital letter and ends with a full stop or similar pause mark, such as a colon (:), semi-colon (;), question mark (?), or exclamation mark (!). Examples –

> *He is walking.*
> *Come over here, please.*
> *Yes.*
> *I love you.*
> *Do you love me?*
> *Certainly not!*

The above are **simple sentences**: they say only one thing, and have only one verb (or occasionally no verb, as in *Yes* or *Certainly not!*) But they *SAY* something.

A **phrase** is a group of words *without* a verb. It makes no sense by itself, but needs something more before it becomes a statement or a question:

> *Above the stairs...*
>
> *Unlike my uncle...*
>
> *A truly wonderful experience...*

A **clause** is a group of words *with* a verb. There are two kinds –

• *Main clause* can stand on its own without anything else to give it completion –

> *(As I came down the stairs)* <u>I fell on my face.</u>

Even if we dropped the coming down the stairs, the falling on my face would still make sense.

• *Dependent clause* has a verb but makes no sense on its own, but *depends* on the main clause to give it completion –

> *As I came down the stairs...*
>
> *If only you had been here...*

Whoever says this...

Not having been born there...

Note: A dependent clause is also called a **subordinate clause**, since it is secondary or *subordinate* to the main clause which gives it its meaning.

A sentence can be ***simple, compound, or complex*** –

- A **simple** sentence has only one verb --

   The cat <u>sat</u> on the mat.

- A **compound** sentence has two or more verbs, often joined by *and* –

   The cat <u>sat</u> on the mat and <u>vomited.</u>

- A **complex** sentence has its main clause plus at least one dependent clause –

   The cat <u>that ate too much</u> vomited.

Final note: When constructing a sentence, aim to keep dependent clauses to a minimum. When they are really needed, it is better to put them after the main clause. Or break the sentence into two. Too many dependent clauses opening a sentence put the reader on hold, waiting to get the full meaning. Thus –

> In the context of human relations, and, given the circumstances of this case, after all the facts have been taken into consideration, those who, in their wisdom and courage, have undertaken to deal with this matter, have come to the conclusion that, at this point in time, to take any action whatsoever would be inopportune.

Note that the meaning of that sentence is deferred to the very final word, so that the unfortunate readers are kept on hold, if they even stay the course. It would be far more effective if it were broken into a couple of shorter sentences, thus –

> It would be inopportune to take any action right now. This is the conclusion of those who are dealing with the matter, having considered all the facts and circumstances.

In sum, go for short words, short uncomplicated sentences, and short paragraphs. Our readers will bless us for it. They might even read us.

PS: Re the question on page 189 – those words don't exist. I invented them for the heck of it while at university many years ago, where we had a rather abstruse but kindly professor who would occasionally release the text of one exam question in advance. My bogus release spread like wildfire, with students ringing up the prof to say they couldn't understand the question. I even had certain eminent academics try to explain the question to straight-faced me.

A wrong and right media release

The following media release has a number of things wrong. Can you find them? The numbers in square brackets refer to the critique that follows

---

Initiative to find macho man announced

By Joe Soap

An initiative [1] to find Ireland's most macho male was introduced with the official launch of the Popov Award last Tuesday [2]. Details were announced at a reception in Dublin's Metropolis Hotel [3]. Representatives of the Popov Vodka Company were present at the launch as well as many of Ireland's leading drinks purveyors [4].

[5] Irish men are becoming more macho every year. This is reflected in their everyday dominant behaviour, and this is reflected in their choice of really macho vodka, and Vladimir Popov wishes to recognise this progression and in response has created the Macho Man Award [6]. Brand manager Miss Rosa Vronsky said at the launch that she was delighted that Ireland's machos were being recognised by such a distinguished vodka maker [7].

The Popov Macho Man Award was set up by leading Russian vodka distiller Vladimir Popov and is now in its 5th year. Last year the response was unbelievably staggering and this year hopes to be an even bigger success [8].

During the coming weeks Irishmen both north and south will be invited to enter for this competition.. The award will be presented to the Irish male deemed to be the most macho in the country. The final will take place in July, when fifteen finalists will be selected and invited to meet with a judging panel comprised of [9] high profile individuals representing the drinks industry in Ireland [10].

In addition to being declared the Popov Macho Man, the winner will also win a winter trip this January for himself and a guest to the beautiful town of Novosibirsk in Siberia. They will travel 1st class to Moscow, where they will stay for two nights in the city's red-light district before moving on to their five star accommodation in Novosibirsk. The Popov Macho Man will also receive 100 roubles spending money and will have the unique opportunity to tour the winter landscape of Siberia and experience the essence of the world's finest vodka producing region [11].

To be in with a chance of winning the prestigious title, really macho people can enter on line at www.irishmachoman.com, or complete an entry form. Closing date for entries is next Friday [12], and there will be five stages to adjudicating process. The overall winner will be announced by Vladimir Popov himself at a reception in in the Siberia Institute sometime later. [13] 27 March, 2019 [14]

Critique

1. First word should be in capitals.

2. Day and exact date must be given.

3. Venue of the launch irrelevant in the intro, unless important to the story.

4. Guest names irrelevant unless important to story.

5. Should not skip line between paragraphs. Indent paragraph instead. (See page 16.)

6. The 'why' of the story should come later.

7. Utterances of delight, etc, have really no place here (unless, of course, the boss insists).

8. Don't exaggerate. Besides, a year cannot hope.

9. Should be *composed of...* or *comprising...*

10. This should have been the intro. It contains the essence of the story, but could be better written.

11. Should have followed the intro.

12. *Next Friday* is meaningless on an editor's desk. Exact date and day required.

13. Put ENDS in caps and centre it. Also put **For further details contact...** below that, in bold.

14. Date should have been at top of release.

The following is a rewrite one hopes is slightly better –

<u>Media release</u>   *280 words*

> **IN BRIEF: Russian vodka maker Vladimir Popov creates award for 'Ireland's most macho man'**

Wanted: 'Ireland's most macho man'

Dublin, 27 March, 2019. THE hunt is on once again for Ireland's Macho with the Mostest.

Once more the invitations are out for Irishmen of macho disposition to enter or be nominated for the prestigious Popov award for *Ireland's Most Macho Man.*

Presented by Vladimir Popov himself, producer of the best-selling vodka here, the award focuses as much on macho characteristics as on appearance, company brand manager Rosa Vronsky says.

Speaking at last night's launch in Dublin's Metropolis Hotel [Tuesday, March 26], she explained that the *Popov* macho man will be not only a knock-over, but will be confident and overbearing, as trumpish and putinesque as possible, and will have an interest in domination.

"Irishmen are becoming more sexy and brutal," Ms Vronsky said. "This is reflected in their lifestyles, including their choice of vodka. The Popov *Company* recognises this, and in response has created the *Macho Man* Award."

The award is now in its fifth year. The five finalists in a ten-stage process meet in August with a panel of judges from Dublin's drink outlets.

Vladimir Romanovitch Popov himself will announce the winner at a reception in Dublin, on Wednesday, 23 November.

This year's Macho Man also wins a *one-week* winter trip for two to the lovely city of Novosibirsk in Siberia.

It includes first-class travel, two nights in Moscow's red-light district (recommended by President Putin), five-star accommodation in Omsk, 100 roubles spending money, and a winter sleigh tour of Siberia's Gulag Archipelago, to experience the essence of the world's finest vodka-producing region. The runner-up will receive a *two-week* tour of the same region.

Entry forms are available at most off-licence stores, and there is also an on-line entry form on the website, *www.irelandsmachoman.com.*

Closing date is 14 June.

ENDS

For further information contact — Rosa Vronsky or Mary Jane Whoever at the Popov Dublin office. Telephone (01) 123.4567. Email: machoman@popov.ie

Appendix 2

Sample pitch

HERE is a sample pitch to invite an editor to consider a proposed article on painter Henri Matisse:

---

28 February 2019

Dr Slavering Jawes
Arts Editor: Gombeen Monthly

Dear Dr Jawes

Seventy years ago this year the world's most famous convent chapel opened – Henri Matisse's chapel for the Dominican Sisters in Vence. Thousands will flock to see it this year.

I first visited it 20 years ago, and have just been there again, to interview the nuns who look after it. It still enchants. I should like to offer you an 800-word piece on the chapel. It would cover the following:

- The story of Matisse's old age spent with the nuns, and his offer to design their new chapel;

- How Matisse created his famous paper cut-outs with scissors and paper, and then translated them into the stained glass for the chapel;

- The extraordinary effect achieved by the stained glass, filtering light onto the white wall opposite.

I can let you have several stunning colour photos of the chapel interior, which show these effects. I hold copyright to these photos, which I myself took, and for which I would expect to be credited.

I write frequently on art topics and have written previously on the stained glass of France's *Musée de Gemmail*.

If I don't hear from you by this day week (Thursday 7 March), I'll take it that I'm free to offer it elsewhere. I hope that's OK with you.

Kind regards.

Sincerely yours:

Mary Jane Whoever

==

Mary Jane Whoever NUJ

23 Dump Park, Dun Dreary, Co. Dublin. V1101 Y6V2
Mobile: 086234567 Telephone: 7891011.

Appendix 3

Sample feature layout

BELOW is a sample feature which was published in the *Irish Independent*. It was originally in 12pt Times New Roman, but has been scaled down here simply to fit this page. NB. Nowadays this format is only to reassure writer or editor as to what the final result should look like. ***But then it must be reduced to PLAIN TEXT, to be emailed and meet the needs of the commissioning editor.*** See page 106 for how to do this.

SHAME
Rice
29 March 2006
Page 1 of 4

We could reduce road deaths   <u>*800 words*</u>

by linking dangerous driving to sexual inadequacy

Shame could cut road deaths

By David Rice

WE all surely remember that road-safety ad that showed the carefree young driver putting the boot down, slaughtering three people, and bop-bop-bopping that ball from a wheelchair for the rest of his life.

And we will also remember that the ad didn't work—as this year's statistics already witness. It didn't work because it appealed to fear, and fear doesn't work.

This is because the vast majority of dangerous-driving offenders are young males between 20 and 35, and young males of that age feel immortal and invincible. Therefore fear cannot reach them.

/more

As Eddie Shaw put it: "Bravado, peer pressure and a sense of invincibility often lead young men to take risks while driving, without realizing the dangers of these risks."

If then fear does not work in the promotion of road safety, what other factor could we call on? *I suggest we try shame.* Social controls have always included fear, shame and guilt, but shame is the one that most powerfully affects young males, for whom the macho image is paramount.

There is nothing new about this. Down through the centuries it was shame that forced young men to fight duels, and it was the shame of cowardice that led many to lose their lives.

However today we could use that same shame to *save* lives. It would slow down a lot of young men if we could suggest that dangerous drivers are shamefully wimpish at bedtime—in other words, *if we could establish a link between dangerous driving and sexual inadequacy.*

But is there such a link? As a matter of fact there is. A 1998 study completed at Exeter University, on behalf of the Devon and Cornwall police, has found such a link—bad drivers make bad lovers, the report says, and aggressive drivers are wimps in bed (*The Sunday Times*, May 3, 1998).

"They have a poorly integrated sex life," says psychologist Chris Burgess, who did the report. "They won't give—they will only take."

That of course includes taking lives.

I would suggest that the Road Safety Authority exploit this link, in an advertising campaign aimed at slowing through shaming. Imagine a series of billboards along our highways with slogans like "Speed is all he gets up!"—or— "High speed, low willy!"

/more

228

I am in no way trying to be funny. And if I am recommending vulgarity, the answer is that vulgarity beats death any time. If vulgarity gets attention and saves lives it will have been well worthwhile.

A couple of years back, in a talk on Five-Seven Live, I made exactly the same proposal, and I was astonished at the response I got, and at how many people believed such a proposal could work. But alas, no one in the National Safety Council took it up. I am still convinced it would be worth a try.

The objective of such a campaign would be to create a permanent "snigger factor", where any attempt at speeding or dangerous driving would invariably provoke jibes about sexual prowess or lack of same. A cultural change, in other words. I can visualise a television ad where a young driver pulls across the white line and roars up the wrong side—and the girls in the back seat start sniggering at him and making snide remarks about the previous night.

Young men fear losing face more than anything. And any ad campaign that would make fast drivers lose face might stop them losing lives.

We've tried everything else—fear, guilt, remorse—none of the other social controls have worked when it comes to road safety. The only one we haven't really tried yet is shame. And yet it is one of the most powerful social controls of all. Since the time of the *Iliad* it has sent young men to war; it created the European culture of the duel and the Japanese culture of *hara kiri;* it enforced chastity upon generations of women here in Ireland (remember pregnant women being read from the pulpit?); it is at the root of the death-before-dishonour attitude that has controlled young men from time immemorial.

/more

Shame can be used for good or ill, but its power is undeniable. And this is one instance where it could be used to save lives. We should be grateful to Exeter University for linking dangerous driving and sexual inadequacy, and we should now exploit that link shamelessly to save lives.

I think we all suspected the link anyway, even if we never put it in words. The French Canadians did, by the way. They have the saying, *Grosse Corvette, petite kiquette*.

ENDS

David Rice is a graduate in Sociology and Community Development, and directs the Killaloe Hedge-School of Writing. His books include... *etc*

A template for feature format

We have created a template for you to get your feature into the standard format (like the above piece). Just google the following –

http://bit.ly/2oqq2AE

<   Or you can use this QR code if you prefer

About the author

A NATIVE of Co Armagh, David Rice has worked as a journalist on three continents. He has also been a Dominican friar. In the 1970s he was an editor and *Sigma-Delta-Chi* award-winning syndicated columnist in the United States, returning to Ireland in 1980 to direct the Rathmines School of Journalism (later DIT). During the following year he also worked as a sub-editor with *The Irish Times* on the invitation of editor Douglas Gageby. In 1989 he was invited to Beijing by the Thomson Foundation to train journalists on behalf of *Xin Hua*, the Chinese government news agency, and to work as an editor with *China Features*. He was in Beijing during the massacre of Tiananmen Square, and later returned to resume his journalism training. However he also secretly interviewed 400 of the young people who had survived the massacre. This brought him to the attention of the Chinese security police, and led to two books, *Dragon's Brood: Conversations with Young Chinese* (HarperCollins), and the novel, *Song of Tiananmen Square* (Brandon/Mt Eagle). His books have been published in Britain, Ireland, Germany, Italy and the United States. Rice's No.1 best-selling *Shattered Vows* (Michael Joseph/Penguin) led to the acclaimed Channel 4 documentary, *Priests of Passion,* which he presented. Rice has degrees in both Sociology and German Language & Literature from the National University of Ireland; in Community Development from Southern Illinois University, Carbondale, USA; and in Theology from the Angelicum University, Rome. He now lives in Co Tipperary, has taught Writing Skills at the University of Limerick, and has directed the Killaloe Hedge-School of Writing for almost 20 years *(www.killaloe.ie/khs).*

Press comment on books by David Rice

The Dragon's Brood

(HarperCollins)

David Rice's *Dragon's Brood* is a marvellously fresh and immediate evocation ... He has a good journalist's sense of the core of a human character, and a gift for asking questions... His book achieves real depth. The belief that the Chinese care little about individual or human rights... should not survive these pages. Rice's eye is sharp and he has useful things to say about many important topics.

—Mark Elvin in the London Review of Books

Illuminating recorded conversations... with explorations of young people's views on all the issues which have been at the forefront of change. Rice's view of China is not a cheerful one...yet he maintains a justifiable spark of optimism.

—Colina Macdougall in The Times Literary Supplement

David Rice makes worthwhile reading... He accurately conveys the often touching despair of most Chinese surveying the wasteland of their recent past. He cleverly invokes their alternating pride in China's size and cultural heritage and their own sense of inferiority towards richer and freer westerners.

—Jasper Becker in The Times (London)

Where Jung Chang leaves off, David Rice takes over.

—Simon Scott Plummer in The Tablet

This intriguing book opens a wide window on the future which before long we will all have to meet and greet and mingle with... fundamental impression of truthfulness... my respect for an enjoyable, enlightening and important book.

—Tony Parker in The Sunday Times

David Rice has done a commendable job in capturing the spirit of the times.

—John Kohut in the South
China Morning Post (Hong Kong)

I trust this book, because of what it says about Chinese faces.... Rice is a keen observer.

—Jonathan Mirsky in The Irish Times

The Dragon's Brood is a singular review of the thoughts and aspirations of a new generation of a people the West has too often misunderstood at its peril.

—Howard Rose in the Sunday Press

Song of Tiananmen Square

(Brandon/Mount Eagle)

Rice has written a gripping and all-too-realistic novel about the Tiananmen Square massacre and the events surrounding it.

—Lord Patten, last Governor of Hong Kong

Utterly fascinating... powerfully affecting... lyricism and immediacy.

—Robert Farren in The Irish Times

David Rice has recreated the sights, sounds, smells and, above all, the emotions of Beijing in the spring of 1989.

—*Jonathan Mirsky,*
who reported the Tiananmen Square massacre
for The Observer

Shattered Vows

(Michael Joseph/ Penguin; William Morrow NY;
Blackstaff; Triumph Books; Ligouri Press)

Despite the anguish it portrays, *Shattered Vows* is an immensely heartening and encouraging book.

—*Robert Nowell in The Sunday Times*

Well documented and at the same time an outcry for changing the present disastrous policy.

—*Professor Hans Küng*

The unmistakable force and vividness that only real life can yield... The fruits of this patient listening are pictures we can see, and voices that speak to us.

—*Professor Uta Ranke-Heinemann,*
University of Essen, author of Nein und Amen

A call for candour on celibacy.

—*The New York Times*

This courageous exposé... provides powerful testimony. David Rice cannot be commended enough for his brilliant study.

—Carol J. Lichtenberg in the Library Journal (US)

I know no study... that compares with this. No one has researched the subject as well as David Rice. No one has listened... with such wisdom and sympathy.

—Peter deRosa, author of Rebels;
Vicars of Christ & others

His book has the convincing ring of truth... conveys an authentic impression... a very sensitive appraisal.

—Dr Joyce M Bennett in the
Church of England Newspaper

This book starkly says the Church is in crisis. Its author is well placed to know.

—Michael Brown in the Yorkshire Post

Kirche Ohne Priester

(C. Bertelsmann; Goldmann Verlag: German translation of Shattered Vows)

A book without hate or rancour and an important contribution to the celibacy discussion.

—Kronen Zeitung

Rice has established a well-founded scrutiny of the present situation.

—Braunschweiger Zeitung

The Pompeii Syndrome / La Sindrome di Pompei

(Mercier Press) (also translation from Newton Compton, Rome)

The Pompeii Syndrome really grabbed me from the first page... it makes you wonder whether we really are in denial about catastrophic threat, because we refuse to believe in the possibility of our own extinction. My test of a good book is always the same - would I loan it to a friend with the proviso that they have to give it back? This definitely meets that criterion.

—Brenda Power in The Sunday Times

The Pompeii Syndrome is a genuinely terrifying, totally believable novel, because it could come true tomorrow ... What sets the story apart is the huge amount of research which underpins every paragraph. Rice has spent years studying the situation. He tells us - as the politicians never do - exactly what we can expect if we do not force our governments to change their policies before it is too late. Run, do not walk, to the nearest bookshop and buy a copy. Better still, buy copies for your friends as well.

—Morgan Llywelyn,
author of The Greener Shore; Grania;
Red Branch & others

A taut thriller... scarily believable. *The Pompeii Syndrome* is fastpaced and explosive... page-turning and thoughtful – a must-read thriller.

—Cathy Kelly, author of Lessons in
Heartbreak; Past Secrets & others

Read this book or regret it till your dying day – which could be very soon...

Brilliantly narrated ... this is no ordinary novel, but 'fiction based on fact'... graphically portrays one route to mass destruction and the end of civilization as we know it. The 'Pompeii Syndrome'... may well enter the vocabulary alongside terms such as 'Stockholm Syndrome'. It refers to... denial in the face of impending catastrophe too awful to contemplate.

An absolutely gripping read.

The unthinkable becomes obvious. The moment when the obvious turns into reality, it is too late. And yet nothing changes. David Rice is the first one to put into words what many see coming but no one wants to see. Of course not. It would mean that something has to change. Now.

The Rathmines Stylebook

(Folens)

We are writing to be understood, and this book will help. Keep what you write simple and short and you can't go wrong.... When in doubt, refer to *The Rathmines Stylebook*.

—*Douglas Gageby ,former Editor, The Irish Times)*

Blood Guilt

(Blackstaff Press)

One of the best-timed releases in modern publishing. David Rice had no idea that in the very week of its publication the central question posed by the book would be on the lips of thousands... What becomes of a gunman when his killing days are over?

—*Evening Press*

The great strength of this novel is that it is in no way mawkish and escapes the sentimentality so many people associated with the 'struggle'. The central character is sufficiently authentic to have the reader identify with his personal odyssey. *Blood Guilt* is an insightful, imaginative and well-crafted novel... Highly recommended, especially for those who appreciate the difference between style and pretension

—*Connacht Tribune*

\#